this book belong to
n. molesworth
St Custards
England
Europe
The World
The universe Space

WHIZZ FOR ATOMMS

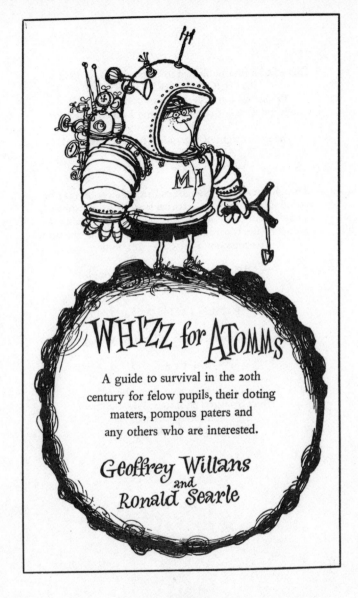

WHIZZ for ATOMMS

A guide to survival in the 20th
century for felow pupils, their doting
maters, pompous paters and
any others who are interested.

Geoffrey Willans
and
Ronald Searle

PAVILION

This edition first published in Great Britain in 1992 by
PAVILION BOOKS LIMITED
196 Shaftesbury Avenue, London WC2H 8JL
Copyright © Geoffrey Willans and Ronald Searle 1956

The moral right of the author has been asserted.

Cover designed by Bet Ayer

A CIP catalogue record for this book
is available from the British Library.

ISBN 1 85145 960X

Printed and bound in Great Britain by Clays Ltd

2 4 6 8 10 9 7 5 3 1

This book may be ordered by post
direct from the publisher. Please contact
the Marketing Department.
But try your bookshop first.

Molesworth ography

In 1951, about the time I had decided to abandon drawing St Trinian's, D.B. Wyndham Lewis – always ready to stick his neck out – suggested that we should collaborate on a St Trinian's romance. His *alter ego* 'Timothy Shy' would write a story if I would agree to do the pictures. I decided to have this last fling and made the drawings, which confirmed to me that I was sick to death of the subject.

The Terror of St Trinian's appeared in October 1952. By Christmas it had sold around 45,000 copies, and Max Parrish, its publisher, urged us to follow up the success at once with a sequel. Wyndham Lewis was keen, but not me, and I refused.

To cheer up a despondent Max, I rashly promised that he should have a better best-seller for the following Christmas. The promise was kept.

Shortly before my meeting with Max Parrish, a journalist friend, Geoffrey Willans, then working with the BBC European Service, had asked whether I could help him put together – and even find a publisher for – a book about schoolboys (groan). Geoffrey had written an occasional series for *Punch* in the Forties, based on his experiences as a school teacher. It was written through the myopic eyes of one Nigel Molesworth, later known as 'the curse of St Custards'.

What Geoffrey had given me to read I finally got round to reading and (surprise) I thought it madly funny. With Max Parrish in mind we set about shaping the idea into a book and I took the result to Max. He wasn't exactly overwhelmed, but finally agreed to take it on for an advance of £300 between Geoffrey and myself, provided I would illustrate the text as 'profusely' as I had the St Trinian's book.

In less time than it takes to produce a baby, *Down With Skool* appeared, and between October and Christmas 1953 had sold 53,848 copies. The saga of The Curse of St Custards was away.

Before Geoffrey died of a heart attack in August 1958, at the ridiculously young age of 47, an anthology – *The Compleet Molesworth* – was already in proof, comprising by then three best-selling volumes and most of a fourth to come the following year – *Back in the Jug Agane*.

Like *The Compleet Molesworth, Back in the Jug Agane* was published after Geoffrey's death. Molesworth joined St Trinian's on the Elysian playing fields and that was the end of school(girl or boy) drawings for me.

Sad that Geoffrey is not around to see the phoenix arise after a quarter of a century of hibernation ect ect chiz moan drone. But whilst he lingers up there in Universt Space (hello clouds hello sky) Nigel is his worthy spokesperson AS YOU WILL SEE. Nowe read on . . .

Ronald Searle

CONTENTS

CONTENTS (CONTINUED)

Prefface

Conoisuers of prose and luvers of literature hem-hem may recall that some of this hav apeared in that super smashing mag *Young Elizabethan*. [ADVERT]. In compiling the present volume it has been my intention insofar as it be within my poor ability – posh stuff this posh stuff go it molesworth – infarso as it be i.e. wot i want to sa is that i hav joly well tried to give others the fruits of my xperience at skool and also of the various chizzes which take place in the world outside the skool walls.

My thanks are due to grabber for the use of his blotch, peason whose pen i pinched and the skool gardener for cleaning out the ink wells – a task which only a man with iron nerve can perform. i gratefully acknowledge the kindly help and encouragement of gillibrand, a most lively source of material ha-ha the dere little wet. molesworth 2 was just about able to read the proofs and pass the speling. You hav to get in a lord or somebody to show you mix in the right company. may i therefore mention Crosby-kershaw-Parkinson, Hon. the A.P.R., who is the absolute dregs and hav had no conection with this book at all?

It is now my pleasure to introduce a few of the sordid felow workers who appere in this book.

N. Molesworth

Perlice Notise

The folowing weeds are known for their long records of crime. Many are completely desperate in every sense of the word, all the others are hopeless. All hav been known to zoom along passages at speeds of

1 PEASON (known as the wet-weed, clot, darling timothy, that boy there ect.)

RECORD Known to be desperate during prep, particularly when he hav been looking at the "Charge of the Light Brigade" for nearly 2 hours. A dead shot with the ink dart. From time to time uters wolfish cries.

DISTINGUISHING MARKS Several beetles drawn in ink on the left knee.

REMARKS He is my grate frend so i hav let him off litely. He is much worse than this aktually as his mummy call him 'darling' and kiss his ickle-pritty face. The old gurl must be blind. Or bats. Or both.

2 MOLESWORTH 2, MY BRO.

RECORD His career read as a case-book for a loony-bin. He zoom about the place going ahahahahahah and pretending to be a jet bomber. Caried out the famous hit-and-run raid on the skool larder. Served sentence in sick wing. Adicted to the arts. His piece "Fairy Bells" on the skool piano will never be forgoten by those who hav heard it.

DISTINGUISHING MARKS He do not share the charm and good looks of his elder bro, molesworth 1, hem-hem. Strange that they could be related. One so fare, the other ugh!

REMARKS Nil.

8

Perlice Notise

mach number, to jab compasses, make aple pie beds, bomb the skool dog, call each other uncouth names, smoke cigs and rob the larder of skool cheese and sossages. If sighted dial 999 or run like blazes.

3 HEADMASTER GRIMES (alias old Stinker, diamond jack, soho sammy and Cave, here he comes)

RECORD A monster of calous cruelty who fly into a bate at every oportunity. Known to consort with desperate carakters on the staff e.g. sigismund the mad maths master. They too hold him in fear.

DISTINGUISHING MARKS A livid scar across the face sometimes looking like a smile, or

REMARKS If anyone can give him 6 months the whole skool will cheer.

4 GRABBER

RECORD Born of very rich parents, and head of the skool. He hav won every prize, including the mrs joyful prize for rafia work. Brilliant at work. Will get a skol. Superb at games. Strikt but fare.

DISTINGUISHING MARKS A coutenance of rare charm.

REMARKS Recieved the sum of 5/– for writing above

N.M. ....orth

1

HOW TO BE A
YOUNG ELIZABETHAN

No one kno wot to do about anything at the moment so they sa the future is in the hands of YOUTH i.e. some of the weeds you hav just seen. As if they kno wot to do about it at their age. All the same we are young elizabethans and it can't be altered – i expect drake felt the same way. Supose we had lived then, eh? i wave my ickle pritty fairy wand, slosh peason with it and the SCENE changes into something most wondrous fair hem-hem i don't think.

Look at me coo er gosh posh eh? You wouldn't hav thort a pair of bloomers would make all that diference. Fie fie – the grown ups canot kno what a privilege it is to be YOUTH in this splendid age of Queen Bess – when all are brave proud fearless etc and looking with clear eyes at the future. (Not so clear after some of those evenings at Court, i trow, when all drink BEER.) All the same it is up to us boys becos the grownups hav made such a MESS of it all. So here i am looking like a hem-hem fule but fearing absolutely O. no one could be so brave. Hist! Hist tho! – i hear the headmaster advancing *clump-clump* with his huge feet encased in gooloshes. I had better begone like a scalded cat. The headmaster is not a young elizabethan he is an old – conduct mark (swearing rude words general uncouth behaviour and letting down the tone of st. custard's.)

OLDE TIMES

Drake, you kno Drake who singed the king of spane's beard, he was the kind we ought to model ourselves on.

Look at me coo er gosh posh eh? You wouldn't hav thort a pair of bloomers would make all that diference

With him he had a gay band of cut-throats who would make molesworth 2, peason, grabber gillibrand ect look like the weeds and wets they are. These cut-throats were very fond of Drake and when he was dead they kept calling to him.

CUTTHROATS: Captin art tha sleeping there below?

DRAKE: How can i when you are making such an infernal din?

CUTTHROATS: Drake is in his hamock —

DRAKE: i am not in my hamock curse you. All there is down here is sea-weed and shells it is worse than a bed in the skool dorm.

CUTTHROATS: Captin —

DRAKE: Wot is it? if you're going to sa 'art tha sleeping' i shall hav insomnia.

CUTTHROATS: Then you are not dreaming all the time of plymoth ho ——?

DRAKE: if i could dream at all it would be of marilyn mun-ro oh-ho that is a good one twig?

(*the cutthroats go home in disgust to fill in their foopball pools.*)

Aktually Drake was pritty tuough and did more or less as he liked espueshully if there were spaniards about. Good Queen Bess was very keen on him in spite of the remonstrances of the king of spane who had a lisp like all spaniards.

THE KING OF SPANE: i tha, beth, that thcoundrel drake hath thinged my berd agane.

ELIZABETH: (*wiping her fhoes on his cloke*) La coz you furprise me you fimply make me rigid.

THE KING OF SPANE: Tith twithe thith week. Ith abtholutely off-thide.

ELIZABETH: Off-fide? Where are your fectaclef? He was on-fide by fix yardf.

THE KING OF SPANE: Yar-boo. Thend him off.

ELIZABETH: Upon my foul tif clear you do not kno the rules of foccer.

(*Raleigh, the earl of essex, john and sebastian cabot join in the brawl with vulgar cries. Which match are you looking at? Pla the game, ruff it up ha-ha etc.*)

What would happen to Drake today?

DON SEBASTIAN ORSINO JERETH DE LA FRONTERA
(*a courtier*): How common!

They were certainly swashbukling adventurers in those days
and life in general was tuougher than an end of term rag at
skool. But it is all very well it is not the same today – I mean
what would happen to Drake if he wanted to singe the king
of spane's berd today?

LOUDSPEAKER: Passengers by Golden Hind for Cadiz
please report to the customs.

OFICIAL: Hav you read this card? Hav you anything to
declare?

DRAKE (*trembling*): No.

OFICIAL: No buble gum no spangles no malteaser?
nothing in the nature of a weapon –

DRAKE: Just this pike –

OFICIAL: Did you buy that pike in Britain, Mr Drake?
Hav you an export license? Hav you filled in form 3

stroke D stroke 907? Are you Mr Mrs or miss? Do you possess a dog license?

DRAKE (*on his knees*): Hav mercie.
OFICIAL: Folow the blue lights to the place of execution.

(*A gold ingot fall from Drake's pocket and he crawls away blubbing. Oficial takes up the ingot. He is lawffing triumphantly the skool dog howls a skool sossage stands on its head.*)

THE CURTAIN FALLS SLOWLY

KRISTMAS AT KURDLING

Of course Xmas was still going in those old times and you can imagin how excited the lusty skolars of Kurdling Kollege are as the end of term approaches. They are all in Big Skool becos there weren't very many skolars in that century the boys used to get away with it.

Piktur the scene if you can – 1576 a.d.

molefworth 1 and molefworth 2 are sitting on an old bench staring with leaden eyes at lat. books. Up and down strides Doctor Kurdling and every few minutes he take up a boy and give him 6 with the kane. An ink dart heaved by peason scrape his august nose.

'Quidem telum emmissit?' he sa in voice of thunder.

'Nemo,' sa the whole skool, for they all speke lat.

Doctor Kurdling do not take their word for it and flog the lot. Boys noses are blue and ears drop off with cold chiz it might be almost like skool today. At last porter ring bell –

KLANG–PIP–KLANG–PIP. (The bell hav been cracked on one side.)

After 6 of the best each they dash out into quad where stand the ancient motto of the kol.

> *Quantum ille canis est in fenestra?*
> (How much is that doggie in the window?)

One of the super things about being an elizabethan skoolboy

Franklyn come here bend over

was that so much less had hapened then. I.E. in Hist you
were doing that utter weed perkin warbeck in modern and
advanced study tho let us face it he was just as big a weed
then as he is today. As for Geog they had only just discovered america and were assimilating the fact for wot it
was worth.

All this could make a geog lession with Doctor Kurdling
v. interesting:

KURDLING: it if sayde to be a fact, skolars, that Columbus
hav sayled fo far to the westward that he hav discovered
the americas. In my opinion, Franklyn come here bend
over *WHACK* there if notte *WHACK* a word
WHACK of truth in it –

MOLEFWORTH 1: fir.

KURDLING: The world of course if flatte – flatte as a pan-
cake – and when you come to the edge any fule kno that
you fall over.

MOLEFWORTH I : fir please fir.

KURDLING: let us assume – Cranmer take that pious
expresion off yore face, Wolsey stop scratching, let us
assume purely as a suposition that there are such things as
the americas.

MOLEFWORTH I : fir fir fir fir please fir.

KURDLING: they can be hardly more than a group of
islands small barren uninhabited –

MOLEFWORTH I : fir, you are wrong. America is a conti-
nent a huge powerful nation live there and the pacific
washes the western seaboard.

DOCTOR KURDLING IS CONVINCED

KURDLING: Fie child you speak with conviction. Stand
forth and bend over *WHACK WHACK WHACK
WHACK* ow gosh ow gosh that will teach you not to
alter the ignorance of a lifetime (which all masters
possess).

MOLEFWORTH I (rubbing his bloomers): Semper aliequid
novum, fir, if i may fa fo.

Of course they had xmas then and wizard rags japes pranks
wheezes chizzes when the skool brake up. grabber drive
away in a gold coach fotherington-Tomas in a smart gig
and Jan the Cowman come for molefworth 2 and me on an
old cart horse.

Xmas day is the same and both get 69 copies of skoolboys
diary for 1567 with spaces for personal details. The usual
sort of xmas mail arive – Dere sir unless your account is
payde. But it is a super day with wizard puding crackers
larfter and song.

And so the new year with its resolutions. Noe smoking
(which is easy becos sir w raleigh hav not discovered it yet).
Decide also to give new xmas present to the poor boys –

An Act of Charitee

Inspiration

The gift

Doubt

Exploration

Despair

17

Meanwhile

Here we are at st custards poised between past and future. How far along the road hav we traveled? How far must we proceed? Wot of Livy and J. Caesar? Will Bluebell win the 2.30 at Kempton? Who cares? This is the present and it is up to us to make it as beauteous as possible.

THE FUTURE OR
OAFS WILL BE OEUFS

Everyone kno wot we are like now you hav only to look around and see it is ghastley enuff. But wot of the future, eh? Wot are we all going to be like in a few centuries? Come on molesworth i have told you a 1000000000 times .....wot of the future?.....come along boy.....how many more times *WAM* hav i *SOCKO* got to tell you *BIFF BAM* that we must never resort to FORCE *WAM BIFF BAM*.....

Wot else? Wot hapens when we get beyond contemporary verse in the classroom e.g. it was the skooner hesperus that sailed the wintry sea and the skipper had taken his little hem-hem to bear him company etc. Well everyone use their branes so much that in the end they are all going to turn into eggs becos they will hav thort a way of getting along without walking. This will not be until 21066 a.d. (approx.) but it makes you think a bit.

And where will the sports comentaries be?

Here come the eggs of 761 st. custardhuss.....they look tremendously fit.....they all hav their log books.....brown and shiny, curled up at the edges.....i see that one of the players hav writen 'if my name you wish to see turn to p. 103 – ha–ha – that used to be done hundreds of years ago.....and now there's a tremendous cheer as of porridge court 979...... THIS should be a grate match.....now they're kicking a few logarithms about and at the other end they're runing over the reactions involving the recombination of ions before the whistle go for the start.....

As a mater of fact it is all quite pappy becos all thinking is done with a machine e.g. the molesworth-peason electronick brane Mark VI which any fule kno was invented by those 2 grate pioneers to do multiplication and long div for them and thus fool sigismund the mad maths master and others of his kind. The early Mark 1 brane that these intreppid inventors achieved was just a simple digital computor working with electric pulses. (I won't explane further as the masters sa when they don't kno the answer.) The brane soon became involved in the study of super-sonic flite and all went well until molesworth 2 creep up and ask it a cunning question e.g. brane, wot is 2+2 eh? At this the brane larff so much that it bust into a trilion pieces.

The œufs of the future, however, are fitted with the much superior Mark VI electronick brane and you can imagine wot it is like in skool.

Scene. A classroom of the future. Twelve branes sit at there desks sploshing infra-red ink at each other. The head eggs helicopter is heard approaching despite its speshul silencing device.

AN OEUF NEAR THE DOOR: Cave! Hear comes the Pukon!

All look keen and inocent.

HEAD BRANE: Today we will do a little comon computing.
8765 MOLEGRUB 1: It's relativity sir not.....

(The automatick kaning machine deliver 6)

HEAD BRANE: As i was saing. Now wot is the polynomial equation of degree n in one variable or unknown....?
LES OEUFS: *(in chorus)* $a^0x^n + a^1x^{n-1} + a^2x^{n-2} + \ldots + a_n - 1^{x+a}n = 0(A. \neq 0.)$
HEAD BRANE: A very nice little rational integral equation –
8765 MOLEGRUB 1: Sir please sir it really is relativity –
HEAD BRANE: Write out the law of electromagnetic induction 5000000000 times.

8765 MOLEGRUB 1: *(thinks)* $D = 1 + \left(\frac{s-1}{npq}\sum_{i=1}^{\overset{w}{}}p_1 - p\right)^2.$

molesworth 2 zoom down with his rotors whirring

The head brane drone on until brake when cocoa and buns are fed in on a conveyor belt and we are allowed to pla around on big field with our helicopters.

'Lets go to mars,' sa fotherington-Tomas. 'Come on molesworth o you mite. We can go up there and hav a lovely think.'

'No,' i sa, 'i hav thort myself stupid already.'

molesworth 2 zoom down with his rotors whirring.

silly sossage can't think for toofee, he sa and zoom away. If only it were like the old days when the tuougher you were

the more you were respected chiz! Now it is the opposite
and if you can't think they all buly you espeshully fotherington-Tomas who hav a huge brane. But there is no hope.
It is 200000 years ahead and I am still learning 'amo'.

'You are a clot-faced wet,' sa fotherington-Tomas,
aiming a thort at me. 'Thou canst not hurt an insecta
siphonaptra or comon flea.'

No wonder i sigh for the old days as we oeufs hav it in
our spechul hist. broadcasts and telyfilms. e.g.

PLAYS FROM HIST

*This illustrates a well-known incident in the uranium age of
the 20th century.*

*Musick: The Gondoliers. Scene: A dorm at st. custards.
Enter molesworth the gorila of 3B cursing.*

MOLESWORTH: who are these weedy ticks who lay their
golden locks upon their pilows? I will uterly bash them
up until their own maters whose fotos grace these sordid
shelves will not kno them. Charge!

(*Comentator:* Observe the low beetling brow the hair which hang
over the eyes, the knees with noughts and croses scribled on
them in ink. What a short step is this specimen from the ape chiz
chiz chiz. What progress hav we made.)

In the dorm pilows fly about in clouds of feathers.

A SKOLAR: Cave! *As they all rush back to bed the* HEAD-
MASTER GRIMES *enter.*

(*Comentator:* This horid creature is no beter than the boys. Look
at him if you can bare it. It make you think do it not? To think
that an objeckt like that could hav thort to teach boys cheers
cheers cheers. In his right hand he grasp wot was known in those
days as a kane or swish, his face is contorted in fury. Such
barbarism o woe o woe it is enuff to bring tears to the eyes.)

The HEADMASTER GRIMES *look around the dorm and sa:*
'Any boy who was out of bed to own up.' *Silence.* 'Curses'
sa head master 'i could hav sworn i heard something perhaps
it was the matron plaing darts againe.' *A well-aimed tomato
hit him in the face.....*

(*Comentator:* Do you see that, eggs eh? In those dark days skools
were full of mutiny and disorder. The pupils ran wild with
wizard wheezes jokes and pranks. They aktually throw a
tomato at the headmaster.....*PING*.....Wot egg did that?
.....Own up or i shall kepe the whole clutch in.....*CRASH
WAM BONK*.....i saw you oeuf 8765 molegrub.....do
not deny it.....you shall hav half an hour in the automatick
kaning machine.....as i was saing it make you sigh to think
of the misery and injustice of those prehistorick times ect. ect.)

The next part of the film show a game of criket but as this is
still going on all cheer. There may be a result by 15678 a.d.

'Curses' sa headmaster 'i could hav sworn i heard something'

2

THE UGGLY TRUTH

The scene is still the dark, doom-haunted skool of st. custards chiz chiz moan drone where the tiny pupils live a life of friteful sufering at the hands of the headmaster GRIMES and his band of thugs who hav the impertnence to call themselves masters.

GRABBER, dark, dashing debonair (compliment hem-hem he is perfectly weedstruck actually) is head of the skool. He is approached one day by a foul-looking specimen called PEASON who is my best friend.

'Look at ickle pritty baby,' sa peason in mocking tones. He run away and not before it is time becos the skool is on fire.

Terible cries come from the roof where MOLESWORTH 2, and FOTHERINGTON-TOMAS, the skool gurly are traped on the roof with the matron and a string of skool sossages. Who will save them? The crowd parts for a mysterious figure which zoom headlong into the fire on his erand of mercy – it is me MOLESWORTH 1, the gorila of 3B, the masked clot. (wot is the use of writing a book if you don't give yourself a good part, eh?) In 5 minits he hav saved the LOT which is pritty good work. Begrimed and exorsted he is aproached by the headmaster. 'Your face and hands are filthy,' he sa. 'Go and wash, boy. Do also 500 lines.' Smarting under a sense of injustice MOLESWORTH 1 decide to run away but, before he can turn, a voice sa 'Stop! Stop him!' It is SIGISMUND THE MAD MATHS

MASTER who point an acusing finger. 'There,' he sa, 'is the boy who start the fire. I saw him do same.' Wot will hapen to MOLESWORTH? Is the can of petrol inflammable? Who hav tampered with the headmasters protractors?

(Now read on.)

'Nearer and nearer crept the ghastly THING'

For story turn to p. 1096b, col. 2.

A GRIM SUBJEKT

CLANG-PIP. CLANG-Pip.

The craked tones of the skool bell sumon all weeds and skolars to xsemble in big skool. This is most unusual just before brake and in the middle of lessons. 'Wot can it mean?' ask grabber.

'It mean,' sa molesworth 2 litely, 'that 99 sparrows hav fallen from their nest in the bell, the masters are interupted doing their foopball pools, the skool dog will eat the buns and – and – '

'Yes? Yes?'

'It mean that thou, o weedy clot, are the biggest wet of them all.'

With this riposte molesworth 2 ignite the fuse and zoom vertically up in rocket flite to safety as HEADMASTER enter. Silence you can hear a pin drop.

'molesworth 2, were you the boy who sai *ZOOSH* as i entered with the staff?'

'Yessir.'

'Can my ears hav deceived me when i heard you calling up mars?'

'Yessir – nosir – yessir.'

'A remarkable feat, molesworth 2. You should be congratulated. Kindly do fifty lines.'

Bad luck aktually getting cobbed but such is the fate of all pioneers. Now to the business of the meeting. HEADMASTER look stern. Tremble tremble quake quake. Wot can it be? Air is blak with sins rising before boys eyes.

SILENCE

'St. custards,' sa HEADMASTER, 'hav always prided itself upon its long tradition of

good maners
discipline
decorum   } *strike out word*
honour   } *which do not aply*
sobriety
musical apreciation

We are all proud of that. i and the staff (*he gives a con-temptuous look over his shoulder at the sheepish colection of branes and louts behind him*) hav laboured long and hard to preserve it. We have done our best to discourage

gambling
poker   } *strike out words which*
drink   } *do not aply tho sometime*
smoking   } *HEADMASTERS*
gurls   } *use all of them.*

Of corse this is only the beginning. It is not for this that we hav been sumoned. These fine phrases are like when moles-worth 2 pla fairy bells on skool piano – it take a minit or two before it sound like an H-bomb.

HEADMASTER *continue*

'Some boy,' he sa. (This is it. Always is when a head-master sa 'Some boy') 'Last night – or in the early hours of this morning – *some boy* broke out of his dormitory and

strike
out
CRIME
which do
not aply
{
discharged pellets at skool pig.
hung by his heels from the weather cock.
bunged up the drane with a pair of socks.
Scared the matron stiff.
Painted the gymnasium purple.
Raided the larder.

O woe tremble tremble agane. Who can hav been so beastley? Wot cad could hav sunk so low? At first there is a feeling of exquisite relief that it wasn't that little business of dougnuts in the deaf master's mortar board in which you were hem-hem involved. Then you look about at the little cherub faces for the criminal. Who look guilty? ALL of them, which do not get anyone very far.

And the HEADMASTER? His eyeballs pop out his hair stands on end and the fur on his gown emit electric sparks. His face is purple and his hands twitch convulsively. One would judge him to be angry.

'Some boy,' he sa agane, 'is guilty. Let him own up now before the whole skool. Let him admit his guilt. Let him step before his judges.'

Silence

'Come on!' he roar. 'Oo dunnit, eh?'

Silence

There you hav the weakness of his case. The clot hav not got an earthly – i mean, well, lets face it he simply doesn't kno. One should really feel sorry for him. He – well, every boy kno wot is coming next.

IF THE BOY DOES NOT OWN UP THE WHOLE SKOOL WILL BE KEPT IN.

It is not always like that sometimes it is the whole skool given six or fifty lines or made to go to bed at six. But it is always the same principle – the Inocent punished on acount of the Guilty in contravention of paragraphs 2 and 3, Sixth Schedule of Standing Orders on British demoracracy. As any fule kno it is therein stated clearly that a guilty party must be arraigned therto and evidence therunto duly and properly brought hem-hem. Any boy kno that and give us 5 minits alone and this is wot would hapen –

Come on grab him by the neck scrag him give him a chinese bu

him up. Tung Fifth dynasty? You surprise me

DET. INSPECTR THE HON NIGEL MOLESWORTH: Now you kno the rule in cases like this the smallest tick hav to own up. What an exquisite vase Lord Weevil. Is it ming?

A VOICE: Wot hav that got to do with it?

DET. INSPECTR THE HON NIGEL MOLESWORTH: Detectives are very cultured. Come on grab him by the neck scrag him give him a chinese burn beat him up and let him hav it. Tung Fifth dynasty? You surprise me. i would not hav thort that tint of eggshell blue – no matter, tie his hands behind the chair. Now, scum, are you going to own up?

No, o no i am inocent.

O.K. Work him over, butch. Headmasters do not care who is inocent, they only want someone to confess. You will only get 6 with the kane – why hav it both ways? And do not bleed on this rich aubusson carpet which lie upon the floor of Big skool etc.

In the end the victim confess and once agane British justice is served cheers cheers cheers.

Aktually in some cases there is no need for these extreme measures. When the headmaster sa he want to see the boy outside who hav been pinching the raspberries the whole Skool surge to the exits trampling all before them in the rush. But, i ask you, wot petty trifles headmasters get worked up about, eh? A few raspberries, a paltry pair of socks in a drane pipe, tadpoles in the tea – you would think such trivial affairs were beneath their notice it show how mentally undeveloped skoolmasters are.

At this moment HEADMASTER glare round.

'Well, the culprit hav had the good sense to confess. If this horid crime is comited agane he will not get off so litely ect.....'

As he go out deaf master take off his mortar board and 12 doughnuts fall out.

'SOME BOY.....!'

SIX-GUN MOLESWORTH

Peace broods over st. custards, that cloistered seat of learning hem-hem. Grabber the head boy – brave, noble, fearless true as all head boys are—is smoking a furtive cig in the lib as he reads about Jane. Other seniors lie at ease reading the works of c. dickens and sir w. scott which would be a chiz if they were only covers to conceal RUDE BOOKS within. In his study the headmaster gravely peruses SPACE ACE: a boy reaches for the bell to order tea. . . . .

Hopo! Hopo! Hookahey!

Bang!

Ya-hay. Ya-hay.

Crack! 'You're dead i shot you you've got to lie down maplethorpe no you didn't yes i did. . . . .'

'Injuns!' gasps grabber, reaching for his winchester. 'Get the wagons in a circle, corral the ponies . . . . .'

A senior stirs languidly.

'It's only molesworth 2 and fotherington-Tomas plaing with the new bugs. Calm yourself, clot.'

Grabber flushes at his mistake. No one speke but they kno that only a few years ago he also was plaing cowboys. They kno that they were plaing cowboys themselves and they flinch at the recolection. Are such games worthy of the new weedy generation who are to blaze a trail of fearless adventure in the new age?

Inspired, i spring to my feet.

'Chaps, felows, custardians i am dashed if this is good enuff. Are we not meant to be folowing the footsteps of drake, howard effingham and other good men who are sleeping tha' below? Are we not suposed to be making a beter world? This low, vulgar game of cowboys and injuns – beg pardon, indians – ort to be stoped for it teaches the tinies ideas of violence. Shall i therefore tuough them up?'

33

'Do that thing,' sa grabber. 'Knock their heads together squish their ears and hack their young shins until they stop.'

It is a mision after my own heart. i spring to the saddle and joris and he etc i zoom he zooms we zoom all three out into the shrubery where i am greeted with a horid sight e.g. molesworth 2 wraped in a blanket.

'How,' he sa.

'Wot do you mean "how"? it is uterly wet to sa "how" you mite as well sa "when" or "where".'

'How.'

'Look molesworth 2 you mite as well listen becos i shall be a prefect next term.'

'How.'

'A box of cigars to the headmaster 20 players to the masters, 5/– to the matron, bone to the skool dog and a box of chox for the maids. That is how.'

'How.'

i am about to bash him when the situation is saved by 16 new bugs who arive saing bang bang and charging round. The weediest one stroll up and say, 'Howdy, stranger?'

To me!!! The gorila of 3B. My veins stand out like whipcords my fists clench and unclench.

'This game,' i snap, 'must cease. Cowboys are weeds and wetstruck.'

'You're a kinda crazy galoot, pard,' sa the new bug. 'Heck, we'll drill you fuller of holes than a seive. Take my advice stranger and git – git outa town – git.'

The poor pipsqueak must be bats. No other explanation can be possible. Quite mad and so young.

'Tell us why you don't like cowboys,' come the chorus. 'Tell us why you do not like them.'

'How!' sa molesworth 2.

'That's enuff,' i sa. 'i shall go bats also. i do not like cowboys for one reason. When the posse chase the hero he always go up a side turning and they always charge past. That is uterly wet. Q.E.D.'

My veins stand out like whipcords

'Pla with us,' chorus the new bugs. 'Go on molesworth 1 pla with us o you mite. Show us how it is done.'

They dance round me weedily like little gurlies all the same they touch my hart poor weak fule that i am.

'O.K.,' i sa, 'bags be a cowboy . . . . .'

10 mins 20 secs. later

'Wot is yon object with a face like a squished turnip which approaches?'

'i kinda figger its tarzan of the apes. Or mabbe there's a resemblance to Vora king of space. Wot does big chief Blue Nose think?'

molesworth 2 give another grunt.

'How?' he sa.

'Pardners i guess it's grabber.'

'Yep it's grabber O.K.'

Tremble tremble moan drone grabber approche looking tuough. 'Look here ticks there's a jolly sight too much din you will even wake the headmaster which takes a bit of

'Yep, stranger, and he's plenty light on the trigger too'

doing at this hour. Wot are you doing, eh?' He see me and his jaw drop. 'You molesworth, a senior, plaing cowboys?'

'Yep, stranger, and he's plenty light on the trigger too,' sa mapplebeck the new bug. 'Git and skit while the going's good.'

36

grabber fante dead away at such neck. When he come to
he find himself by molesworth 2's wigwam where a huge
pot of radio malt is slowly cooking at the fire. Beyond it a
delicious meal of dried braces and stewed prunes.

'Who are you?' gasp grabber.

'How,' come the chorus.

'How indeed can an apparition so friteful with a blue nose and a smelly old blanket hav come to pass? Wot is it?'

'How.'

'This will drive you crazy, pard,' i sa. 'Join our merry game we are having a supersonic time.....'

5 mins 6 secs. later

'Cave, chaps! Here comes the head. You've woken him up from his hog-snoring.'

Headmaster it is indeed with the skool coyote scampering at his heels and barking. Headmaster is in good bate and chat with the matron about gillibrand's vests hem-hem so he is glad to change the subject when the new bug with specs jump out at him.

'Stick 'em up,' he sa. 'Pronto. And that goes for your squaw too.'

'A game of cowboys,' sa the headmaster. 'An excellent game to develop quick thinking. I trust however that when the hero turns to the right the posse do not galop past? You see it is obviously quite simple – '

'Sir sir sir pla with us sir. Sir pla with us.....'

20000 years later

As i said before, the human race hav progressed so much that they hav only tiny legs and the rest of it look like an egg. they hav so many branes. It is afternoon at the Institute Custardhuss. Sudenly a shout rends the air: 'Tha he goes git after him.' One egg is hotly pursued by sixteen other eggs.....the first egg pulls up a sidetrack to the right and the other eggs go thundering by.....

There is a lesson in this and wot it is i am sure molesworth 2 can tell us. He ponder for several hours and at last give his verdict.

'How.'

MORE CULTURE AND A CLEANER BRANE

Now it can be told. The story of our pioneer inventors early struggles . . . . .

'I think, peason,' sa prof. molesworth, gravely. 'That we may now conect the cyclotron to the reactor. We shall then be ready for the plutonium – '

'You mean ? ? ? ? ? ? ?'

'i do not kno wot i mean, o measly weed. But if all do not go well, i would not give 2d for st. custards chances in the local skools charity league next season.'

Above them tower the huge atommic PILE which they hav constructed in the MUSICK room. There are 10 bombs – a litle one which trigger off a bigger one, which trigger off the next one until you get to the last which is super coolossal.

'Well?' sa prof. molesworth. 'You seme thortful?'

'It is just that it appere to be going to a lot of trubble just to heat the gym.'

CAVE! CAVE MOLESWORTH CAVE!

The warning cry come just in time. HEADMASTER GRIMES puts his hoary head round the door. He beam at the two keen little chaps who are now sitting together at ye olde skool piano plaing a super duet.

'Bravo,' he yell above the din. 'Keep it going, hep-cats, get in the groove. If that is the *Flite of the bumble BEE* it must be the biggest bee in the world, in space. It sound more like a comet IV at full boost. It is louder than when molesworth 2 pla *Fairy Bells*.

'There are 2 of us at it,' shout prof. molesworth. 'Why not join us, sir, on drums?'

'No, no. Can you lend me a tanner till tuesday?'

GRIMES catch the coin in his mortar board with the skill of long practice and withdraw. Out in the passage he rub his hands. 'Peason and molesworth are at last settling down to a sense of responsibility,' he sa. 'st. custard's will hav cause to remember them.'

He pick up his banjo and move to the next pitch outside 3B where he strum *swannee river* with one hand and ratle the bones with the other. Molesworth and peason return to the 'Young Students Chemistry Set' which gran hav given molesworth for Xmas..........

'Wot are you doing, molesworth, go on tell me o you mite.'

It is fotherington-tomas who intrude this time skipping weedily he is utterly wet. And is he to be trusted? Hav he been cleared for security, eh?

'It is the Peason-molesworth Atommic Pile fitted with radio and plug for electric razor.'

'Goody goody,' sa fotherington-Tomas. 'Will it cost a grate deal to get a shave?'

'About three trillion pounds.'

'A new era for the world,' sa fotherington-Tomas. Then he begin to blub. 'Science is not everything. There is culture as well.'

'Come agane?'

'In a mechanised age the things of the spirit are more important than ever. Consider shapespeare, c. dickens, c. kingsley, sir w. scott and others. And wot of christopfer robin, eh?'

His words set up a chain reaction and the skool piano and chemistry set blow up. Only the Peason-Molesworth Atommic Pile seme unaffected tho we use the metronome as a geiger counter.....

That was how it began. That nite in the Pink Dorm i hav DOUBTS. It is the same old q. for a scientist. Should he make his knoledge avalable to everyone? It do not mater one jot in my case becos with my knoledge they would all still be where they were before. And wot about all these

Should he make his knoledge avalable to everyone?

books which we hav in eng.? Wot of all those q's in the exams e.g.

Sa wot you kno of silas marner, queeg, jack the ripper, perseus and mrs do-as-you-would-be-don-by. Writing and neatness will be taken into consideration.

Answer:

A grate thort strike me:

ALL BOOKS WHICH BOYS HAV TO READ
ARE WRONG

How dare you, molesworth. You are idle, inattentive, slovenly, stupid, irascible, hopeless and hav o branes. Also you hav drawn beetles all over m. dubois in the fr. book and hav given armand a moustache.

How dare you?

i can see wot will be the answer to my grate thort but i hav my defence.

Take the first book in my little selection this week e.g. O. Twist featuring in the old Curiosity Shoppe introducing douglas fairbanks jr. as fagin. Book and lyrics by grabber 1. From an idea by c. dickens.

You remember how it go? Where is my book bag? Ah, here it is. O. Twist feel that he hav not had enuff skool sossages ect. and ask Mr bumble the beedle for more i.e. he make the message quite clear and sa Please, sir, can i hav some more. Mr bumble is so surprised anyone could want any more he fall into a rage and O. twist get his chips. Now wot would hapen toda?

TWIST: Another sossage, fatty.

BEEDLE: Eh, wot. You hav had yore allocation as pre-sribed in the skool leaving act A/cD/10L.

TWIST: Come on come on. This is the welfare state. Give us a couple also some free milk and orange juice, a corset, some false teeth, old age pension, forecast for the pools, 20 peoms by w. auden, six beetles, a pencil sharpner and anything else you hav in yore poket.

BEEDLE: No, no.

TWIST: Garn, or we'll rip yer.

It is the same with many a well-known charakter. Another is that well-known weed christopfer robin who luv . poo bear ect. and watch the changing of the gard at buck house with alace, alice, avise alias Mopp the Mess.

ALICE: They are changing the gard at buckinham palace.

C. ROBIN: So wot so wot?

ALICE: You had better be there. You have yore publick. You hav made the whole place impossible for the q, also the de of e and prince charles.

C. ROBIN: i am getting past it i am slipping.

ALICE: You talk as if you hav to march from wellington

baracks every day. *And* carrying a trombone. Where are yore call-up papers?

Another wet in my book bag is jules verne. He said there would be submarines he is brilliant. Also the flying machine e.g. around the world in 80 days (delay at gander even b.o.a.c. must start to be thinking they mite catch up) jules verne, in fakt, was responsible for SCIENCE Fiktion, also h. g. wells who wrote The First Clots in the Moon.
You remember how it went? Or not?

FOTHERINGTON-TOMAS: Hullo clouds hullo sky. Let's all go to the moon. Hurray hurray. Prof. cavour hav the answer i.e. the Peason-Molesworth Space Ship (patents pending).

ZOOSH!

The scene switch to the MOON. 20 mushrooms are on watch. They watch the skies. They also watch each other wondering which will be fried with the bacon and skool sossages tomorow. Sudenly a BALL arive. The mushrooms jump up and down.

'Go on, Stanley, net the leather. Get yore head to it. Foul! Send him off. Shoot! Buy more players. Who's for tennis?' SUDENLY there is a hush.

1ST MUSHROOM: Anything the matter?
2ND MUSHROOM: It's THEM. From THERE.
1ST MUSHROOM: Cripes. Where's THERE?
2ND MUSHROOM: Here's HERE. THERE'S there. THEM'S they. He, she or it equal the 3rd person sing and ushually go in the nomminative.
1ST MUSHROOM: Higgnerant. Here THEY come.
2ND MUSHROOM: Ugh!
MOLESWORTH: (*stepping forth from the space ship*) Ugh!

they glare at each other, mutually repulsive. He canot eat

me for brekfast and i canot eat HIM. Impasse. Nothing for it but to go home.

ZOOSH! ZOOOOO....!

Wot's wrong? Anything the matter? Try the boost. Flog the reactor. Why did i not marry a mechanic? ECT......

And so it prove my point q.e.d. There is only one thing. Tomorow is another day and there will be geom. eng. fr. lat. botany, rest on the bed and then ho for more. Life is tuough. It depends whether you can take it.

2nd Mushroom: It's THEM. From THERE

3

HOW TO SURVIVE IN
THE ATOMMIC AGE

As i sit among my faded memories and old relicks e.g. lat books, bungy, caterpillers, mice and old stamps which i hav not stuck in, wot do i find but my Skoolboy's diary. This tell me that it is 7021 miles from London to Bangkok, also my size shoe is 6 watch number 234547 and oxford won the boat race in 1896 so wot i sa so wot. At this moment fotherington-Tomas skip in –

'O molesworth,' he cri. 'Do read me your diary go on o you mite.'

'Well – ' i sa, flatered in spite of myself.

'Goody goody i hav always admired your prose work altho sometimes it is a little *strong* especially when they set us "Wot i think about masters."'

So the little wet curl up on the floor and i read:

> JAN 1. *did nuthing.*
> JAN 2. *mucked about.*
> JAN 3. *Went to a party.*

'Genius,' cri fotherington-Tomas, claping his hands. 'Economical, stark, compressed t.s. eliot himself . . . . .'

But i do not listen for i think about parties and parties mean gurls chiz chiz chiz . . . . .

All girls are soppy. This fact is recognised by all boys and the mesage is clear but seme to become dimmer as they

45

draw on to man's estate chiz. Eventually it fade altogether and all is lost in a welter of SOP and SLUSH, like you get in the films they dare not show us at Skool. e.g. darling chiz i guess this is the end. Gurl cries tho heaven knos why, she luv other men beter and hav a husband anyway. Man then go into the night from which he should hav never emerged. 'How beautiful,' sa your mum to your pater who is sitting despondently behind her. 'If only you could be noble like that ocasionaly.'

'It is only a world of makebelieve,' he repli. 'You must face up to reality.'

'Reality,' sa molesworth 2, 'is so unspeakably sordid it make me shudder.'

He take a bullseye and pater lite his pipe. The matter is closed.

If we are to believe the books gurls read life at their skools is full of jolity and xcitement. There are always some tremendous PROBLEMS to be solved e.g. 'why choose mavis?' sa the other pres indignantly. 'We doubt her capacity to handle the most difficult house in the skool.' Do they not kno they talk about mavis grabber? grabber ma is head of st custard's and win the mrs joyful prize for rafia work. He could win a brownies kniting badge for the ushual amount.

Anyway imagine wot life would be like at st custard's if the weeds oiks tuoughs snekes and others behaved like they do in gurls books. Imagine conversashuns like this:

'Rats, you crumpet,' sa gillibrand, the mad cap of 3B. 'It's joly rot to sa that molesworth cribbed in the botany exam.'

'It's simply swete of you to sa that, gilly dear,' chime in peason. 'I kno he was cobbed with 3 newts and a titmouse in his gym shirt, that he hav a guide to natural hist open on his desk, a snake curled round the leg of his chair, a pair of binoculars, and british birds tatoed on the palm of his hand – but there must be *some* explanation.' (there is, enuff said.)

The xpresion tense on his luvley face

'And you realise this mean he won't pla in the lax match aganst st Cissy's on Wednesday? Oh bother i do think miss grimsdick is too bad.'

He toss his tawny head and a hale of beetles fall out.

molesworth flush as he enter the study. He know they hav been talking about him becos they wouldn't hav been little gurlies unless they had been jabering,

'Hullo, you clot-faced sewer rats,' he sa, quietly, the xpresion tense on his luvley face, the lights in his hair shining and also the lights on his nose.

'O, moley dear, you absolute juggins! Now miss grimsdick want to see you in her study.' molesworth go chalk white benethe the dirt.....

Aktually my racecourse correspondent tell me that real life in gurls' skools is not a bit like what (grammer) it is in the books.

'Carrots' Crumpshaw, the madcap of the fourth is swanking along to the musick room when a huge prefect bear down on her.

'Crumpshaw! Why are you walking down the Milky Way, a pasage reserved for prefects? *WAM*. And you ar wearing lipstick. *SOCKO*. And you cut the coll. criket match. *BIFFO*. Blow yore nose. (*ZOOSH*). i shall tell the whole house to pinch you this evening. . . . .

('Carrots' Crumpshaw thinks: just becose miss peabody
[gym] praised my knees bend she is jealous.)

'How cynical you are, molesworth,' sa fotherington-Tomas,
at this juncture. 'Gurls can be most interesting companions,
as you will find when you gro older.'

The only bonds in fact between boys and gurls is that the
skools they go to are SIMPLY SHOKING.

N.B. my racecourse correspondent tell me that there are
some gurls skools like ro-hem, st. j-hem, heath-hem, wyk-
hem, where all is luxury and you must bring yore own
servant to tend after yore lightest wants. Imagine this at st.
custard's eh i mean to sa just imagine it.

Dawn brakes a few dispirited birds sa Queek and go to
slepe agane the skool dog growls in his slepe a master steel
guiltily across the lawn. Another day is beginning at st.
custard's.

Tap! a manservant enter with a glass of coca-cola.

it is seven a.m., sir on a filthy morning and all is friteful.
Snore.

The curtains are drawn sir and your clothes are laid out.
Yore marbles are laid out on the closet.
Snore.

The ice in the white jug hav been broken. Should you
wish to clean your teeth or knees the appropriate brushes
are at hand. the electric fire is switched on and before you
lies the adventure of new day. One last word the penalties
for being late for brekker are mediævil in their severity.

SNO – in the middle, the matron burst in like an atommic
Xplosion. Wakey-wakey she bellow, sho a leg rise and shine.
Up you get rats it is only 20 below and there is nothing like
a song before brekfast. . . . .

Another dreme is shatered. Come to think of it, gurls hav
to put up with boys. So their lot is hard too.

How to be a Goody-Goody

A smug chart for sissies
Get teacher to hang this on the klassroom wall

Do not bolt your food, boys. Eric sits erect and chews his food at leisure becos the weed hav got up early.

Now look at nigel, ugh!

49

A FEW TIPS FROM THE COARSE

A velvet silence (peotry) enclose the famous PINK dorm of st. custards. Beyond the curtaned window there is no sound except the tread of feet as boys break out down the fire escape and the plop-plop of darts as ye olde matronne sink another treble twenty into the board. Below a gang of mice attack the skool cheese with jelignite . . . . .

Sudenly the stillness is broken by a low, musical whisper e.g.

Wot is yore fancy for the 3.30 at Sponger's park, tomow, molesworth?

Instantly the whole dorm is awake. Aktualy it was never silent becos wot with SNORES GRUNTS AND GROANS it would be quieter when they are re-laying the surface of the 7 sisters road than here.

The q. i hav been asked, however, catches my interest.

Get out the port and cigars, i sa, and we will diskuss the form. i wate until the decanter is passed hem-hem it is pepsi-cola aktually and give my verdict.

Bees Knees will be having a go. On breeding alone it should be cast-iron. i shall risk half a lb of wine gums on her.

Ta-ran-ta-rah! yell molesworth 2, weedily. 'Come on, lester pigot. come on, scobie breasly. Come on me yar boo to molesworth 1 he couldn't hurt a flea.'

He jump up and down on the soft springs hem-hem of the skool bed until he bounce too high and strike his head on the ceiling cheers cheers.

Which all go to show that apart from backing a county at criket, a foopball team or two, cris chataway, le rouge at the casino and mr grabber for the father's race every boy ort to equip himself for life by knoing a bit about horse racing.

All i kno about this, subjekt is contaned in my grate work *Snaffles, fetlocks, pasterns and girths* – A CRITICAL

This is only one side of a horse

EXAMINATION (Grabber 25/– or send a p.o. to the auther direct). This book go to the hart of the matter by considering something you canot hav a horse race without e.g. the HORSE. (see above)

This is only one side of a horse so it hav only two legs, one ear and one eye. However, most horses are aproximately the same on the other side and if they are not it is not safe to hav a fluter on them.

Every horse is said to hav POINTS which is pritty dificult for any animal which is not a hedgehog or comon porcupine. In racing, however, there are only two POINTS about the horse which need concern the eager student – the ears and the tail. If the horse is going to try the ears should be so far back and the tail so far up that they almost meet. When it trot up to the post like that the backer can be sure it is trying, which is something with a horse. It is something with a boy, too, but no one can kno from his ears otherwise we mite get something like this in klass –

MOLESWORTH 1 *stare at a problem in algy scratching his hoary head.*

SIGISMUND THE MAD MATHS MASTER *regard him anxiously through his racing glasses.*

SIGISMUND: there go the galant molesworth upon whom i hav put my shirt (heaven forbid). He is a cert for this algy problem. But wot is this? His ears do not twitch. He sweateth at the mere look of x+y. He screws his pen into his ear he is in a lather. Quick quick i must lay this off on peason who hav an answer book but it will be O.K. unless there is an objektion.

(*He rushes out. molesworth gets the answer from gilibrand and so foils the plot.*)

That is all about horses. Now the q. is how to put your money on. You do this with a bookie or the tote as even a fule kno. Wot every fule do not kno however is which horse to put the money on and bring back a dividend.

To kno this you hav to study form e.g. buy all the papers which say:

> The Dope's Nap – 3.30. BEES KNEES.
> 3.30. FATTY IS A CONFIDENT SELEKTION.
> COARSE WIRE. 3.30. BUMBLE PUPY.
> NEWMARKET. TOOTHBRUSH.*******

This leave you pritty much where you were but it is better than buying a midday edition when all the tipsters agree:

RACING SUMARY. 3.30.

PREPOSTEROUS (*Daily Plug*)	DANDRUFF
MENDAX (*The Smugg*)	DANDRUFF****
ON THE BALL (*Daily Shame*)	DANDRUFF
ALCESTES (*Farmer's Joy*)	DANDRUFF

ect.

Every horse is said to have POINTS

Everything is right. DANDRUFF hav won over the distance, it hav two ancestors from the national stud, a french owner, trained on meat, sits up in its stable, lest... pig...up...firm going THE LOT. BASH ON THE WINE GUMS. As you are sitting nonchalantly in your club drinking a last pepsi-cola you carelessly pick up the ticker tape.

3.30. SPONGER'S PARK. I. BEES KNEES. 2. CLOT. 3. MORBID. ALSO RAN—DANDRUFF. SKOOL CHEESE. 5 RAN. DANDRUFF 5 I/I ON (FAVRITE)

'Hogsnorton.'
   'Yes. sir?'
   'Bring me another pepsi cola.'
   'The '37, sir, or the Club?'
   'Wot do it matter? There is only 6d in it.'

Let us stroll over to the padock where the horses are parading. All around is the clamour and bustle of the race-coarse full of gipsies, oafs, cads, snekes tipsters, bullies in fakt it mite just as well be a half-hol at st. custards. See who strolls among them it is ickle-pritty fotherington-Tomas the wonky wet of the skool!

FOTHERINGTON-TOMAS: Hullo clouds hullo sky! How colourful the scene! the colours so gay so alive. But, woe, here is the headmaster GRIMES!

HEADMASTER: Want to buy some jellied eels? Lovely jellied eels. (he starteth) Discovered! it is fotherington-tomas!

FOTHERINGTON-TOMAS: Oh wot, sir, can hav brought you to this pass?

GRIMES: the skool doesn't pay all hard work nothing out of it. The boys hav got to be fed and as for the masters they fair eat you out of house and home. (*fotherington-tomas begin to blub*) And then look at the rates on the old place – and the taxes. Can't blame me if i try to make an honest penny down here, there's no disgrace –

FOTHERINGTON-TOMAS (*blubing harder than ever*) don't go on, sir. Take my money. Here.

GRIMES: don't you want no jellied eels?

FOTHERINGTON-TOMAS: no, no.

GRIMES: Bless you, sonny, you hav a kind face.

As fotherington-Tomas skip away a thick wad of banknotes fall from GRIMES poket. He pick them up agane and begin to GLOAT!

PLATE IX   PICK THE WINNER – to face page p. 100076.

GRIMES: there is one born every minit.

And now we hav aktually got to the padock where the horses are walking round and round and people are looking at them. This is yore first chance to make sure yore selektion is in racing trim. Even at this stage it may be lathering and foaming at the mouth. If, however, its eyes are brite pinpoints, it is dancing lite-hartedly on its horseshoes and neighing to itself – it is safe to assume that the stable hav decided to hav a go.

BASH ON MORE WINE GUMS and return, for the START.

This is the most exciting moment and fotherington-Tomas jump up and down.
  'Hurrah hurrah how good it is to be alive and the horse is the frend of man!'
  At this moment a beer botle fall on his head from the roof of a motor coach and he is borne away. Cheers cheers we can watch the race in peace. THEY'RE OFF! Everyone go mad men shout, gurls fante, molesworth 2 shout ta-ran-ta-ra. Everyone shout and point at each other. IT'S BEES KNEES. DANDRUFF A STREET. FATTY WALKS IT ECT. The race only last ten secs before it is over. And wot hav hapened to the chokolate hoops, raspbery hoops and suede gloves of yore fancy? Alas, it is almost always down the COARSE.
  Boys, keep away from race coarses. Wot is the fun of them. They are crooked and you do not stand a chance. Open the paper and see how grave the world situation is. Look at the H-bombs and disasters and find how you can give yore services to the cause. Open the paper i sa – and wot is the first thing that catch yore eye?

> 4.00. COARSE WIRE. NANKIE-POO CAN'T MISS.

BASH ON THE WINE GUMS!!!!!!!!!

THE MOLESWORTH MASTER METER

Chiz moan drone they are everywhere. Masters i mean.
Beaks. Thin ones fat ones little ones tall ones some with
cranky cars others with posh ties, some you can rag and
others who strike mortal fear into our tiny harts it is cruelty
to expose us to such monsters. Everywhere a boy goes at
skool there is liable to be a master chiz chiz seeking you out
with his fierce burning eyes. It was becos of the pressing
need hem-hem for some such instrument that the molesworth Cave-Counter or master meter (patent pending) was
invented. See below.

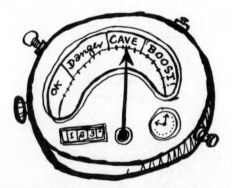

prof molesworth and his batty assistant peason had the
geiger counter in mind in creating their famous master meter.
The principle is the same. When a master is in the offing
dreaming of BEER and LUV the meter throb and the needle
come up to the CAVE position on the dial. Increasing
danger makes the needle creep up until it reach the maximum
spot ie. when a master rush you with a kane held in his hary
hand and his eyes bulging with fury the needle show
BOOST and the whole gadget zoom up and down like a
skool blancmange. That is the time to scram quickly leaving
a heavy pall of cig smoke hem-hem behind, safe and sound
with trousis still full of dust thanks to yore Cave-counter.

In fakt in generations to come the name of molesworth will be venerrated among skoolboys as we are suposed to venerrate the chap who discovered chloroform and other pane savers.

But enuff. Charge ta-ranta-rah for the masters comon room. Leave yore Cave-counter behind or it will go mad at so many masters, such a pong poo-gosh of pipes and cig ends you would almost think they all go around picking up ours.

Any boy kno wot a masters comon room is like. It smell of beetles and the ceiling is suported by ex. books. It is a place where you take yore lines, impots and corections

    e.g.

A stitch in time saves nine
A Stich in save tim
A ssave is nine
   A stitch in time sav
   A stich in tim save

on the table. The master look up from the chair at the fruits of yore toil and sa languidly All right molesworth you can go away now. Then he go to slepe agane while below the slaves are toiling in the salt mines.

Here then the masters gather in their gowns and discuss the problems of their existence i.e. the brave noble and fearless boys whom they persecute. When the HEADMASTER is around this is how it goes.

you kno HEADMASTER that thanks to the brilliance of my tuition, the care i hav lavished, the hours i hav spent molesworth hav improved in lat out of all knoledge.

HEADMASTER (*thinks*) Wot is all this leading up to? i must go carefully.

Of corse 3B were v. backward when they came to me. i am not saing a word aganst popplewell – a sound teacher within his limmits but it took my genius, my inspiration to make molesworth put 3 konsecutive subjects in the nomm.

HEADMASTER: Grand work Grand work.

MASTER: How about a quid until next thursday?

HEADMASTER: (*quickly*) I'm out. Haven't a nicker.

MASTER: Make it arf a crown.

HEADMASTER: Very well. The ushual rates. And i foreclose next week.

Otherwise you can guess wot go on. Every evening a commando course taken by the Sarnt-major and an open space for unarmed combat.

SARNT-MAJOR: O.K. now. Get fell in. Two ranks. By the right – DRESS. (*Shuffle Shuffle* As you were ect the old gag.) Now. We all kno the Hobjekt of our hinstruction i.e. that is how to do the boys proper. No knives no knuckeledusters only a ruler alowed. All right. Fall out number 6, arbuthnot, sigismund, maths master, mad. HIFF you were required to do a job on a boy how would you go about HIT? i see. Very hinteresting but scaracely fare pla. hi do not think as ow we need to go *that* far. Hact haccording to the manual.

ORRIGHT?

(*Fancy asking a lot of MASTERS if they are orright. Haddress the q. to the boys. They'll give you the right answer.*)

SARNT puffs out manly chest and continue humidement:
'Hon the word One Hobserve the boy or pupil who is busy on hillicit hactiivity i.e. has it mite be drawing tadpoles on the blotch. Hon the word TWO – draw hin the hibrows, making sure that the rest of the klass hobserve and hapreciate the umor of the situation.

ORRIGHT?

(*Enuff said.*)

Hon the word THREE – grasp the ruler and stand behind
the boy or pupil with the hands lightly hupon the ips.
Wait for the larff. (Hit is never difficult for a master to
hobtane a larff.) Hon the Word FOUR bring the ruler
down promptly and smartly on the victim's swede. A
howl of pane his the signal that the hobjektive hav been
attained.

And so it go on for Masters kno that if they once relax their
vigilance the DAY IS OURS. JUICE! GLOAT! i can
hardly wate for their shrieks for mercy.

So far we hav dealt only with masters who are english e.g.
sir jones, sir arbuthnot, sir phipps-potts BA sir higgs-hake,
sir muggs f.r.g.s. ect. But, felow suferers, remember this.
There are skoolmasters all over the world, even bulgarian
skoolmasters which take a bit of doing gosh chiz. But before
you think it is hard cheddar on the bulgarian boys remember
this is the atomm age and masters are exchanged like stamp
swaps from country to country.

WE MITE GET A RUSIAN MASTER AT
ST. CUSTARDS!

gosh golly you
can pikture it.

We mite get a Rusian master

Into 3B stump sir petrovitch who not only hav a face like a squished tomato (as all masters do) but hav hary wiskers.

THE KLASS: Good morning, sir petrovitch.

SIR P: good morning, little children. (*He burst out blubbing*) o woe o grief the HEADMASTER makes me teach lat. geog, algy, arith, fr, eng, some carpentry, musick, the organ and asist with criket it is worse than the salt mines. Wot is the lesson, little children?

THE KLASS: peotry, sir petrovitch. (*They recite*)

> *Harkski harkski the larkski*
> *At heavenski's gates singski*

(*sir petrovitch cry more and more*)

THE KLASS: Give him Boots that will slay him.

FOTHERINGTON-TOMAS: o goody!

THE KLASS: Bootskis, bootskis, bootskis movin' up and down agane (ect)

SIR P: Good show good show. Give it the rhythm. Definitely give it the rhythm, dogs.

(*He jumps on the desk with his boots shouting Oi Oi Oi and struming on a balal – well you kno. The whole klass join in – ink wells fly threw the air, the uprore is immense.*)

HEADMASTER look up from the desk in his study where he is counting the GOLD in his moneybox: 'Comrade petrovitch can certanely instil an unwonted enthusiasm into 3B tho his methods are a little – er – unorthodox. Now shall i raise the fees or hav i got enuff? Beter be on the safe side.' He taketh up his gold plume et commence a ecrire: Dere parent, Owing to the cost of living and death-watch beetle in the bell tower i regret ect ect...The tears fall in pools from his eyes, smudging the encre. But that is nothing to wot hapen when the parents receive it. You should hear the WORDS yore pater use when he cancel the order for a rolls-royce and make do with an A90 instead.

So much for comrade petrovitch and the 89 ickle pritty capitalists of st custards.

Now we come to another swap. This is ed. hickenhopper from the U.S.A. of america i.e. he is wot we vulgar boys hem-hem call a YANK. He is very tall and wear specs hem-hem and we awate his appearance with interest i.e. where do he keep his gat?

'Now, boys,' he sa, 'this morning it is lat. We will comence with translation.'

'O.K. Stranger. Hep-hep and get cracking.'

'Do you, molesworth, consider yourself equal to attempting sentence one?'

'Sure don't, pardner. Never was no good at book larnin. Try one of these other critturs who are hog-snoring in the desks around me.'

'Now come,' sa sir hickenhopper. 'Balbus admires the clear voices of the girls – surely now – ?'

'Now listen. i ain't aiming to make no trouble. You're the sheriff around here. But if the mean coyote who wrote that latin book come into this saloon i'll riddle him full of daylight. And the same goes for Balbus.'

And so it go on it is only after a long time that you find out that all YANKS are not cowboys and while you are still reeling with disapointment you learn too that they are not all gangsters. Well, of corse, my dear, that remove their last atraction for me but i expect they hav found it quieter to live at home if they can watch the television instead of shooting all the time. A pity.

Aktually, yank masters are diferent from ours. If sigismund arbuthnot the mad maths master were to organise us into a task force to solve a quadratick equation we would think him mader than ever. But that is wot ed. hickenhopper did. And we rather enjoyed it – wot am i saing *ENJOYED* it? CURSES CURSES. Re-shake this cocktail, peason, and don't drown the gin.

A Wizard Wheeze

ST. CUSTARDS.

Name or Cognomen: Cyril Bertie Cedric de wetby Higgs-Hake, alias Smokiy Joe alias The Creeper.

Age: 102 (approx) **Position:** The Bottom

French: He tries hard at this subjekt and considering he hav never been nearer La France than the front at Margate his ability is remarkable.

Latin and Classicks: He do not sho a grate deal of interest. The extraordinary behaviour of Balbus, Cotta, Caesar and Labienus do not fill him with disgust as they should neither does the appalling mortality rate among the Gauls seme strange. He is inclined to be idle and boring, staring out of the window with his mouth wide open.

English: His idea of instilling the treasuries of english literature seme to be to turn his klassroom into the training camp of some puglist. Howlps of pane, right-upper cuts, biffs and bangs. I fear that he haw not an 'h' to his nafme and it is a case of the blind leading the blind hem-hem.

Manners: Quite revolting.

Why be down-troden? Is this a free country? Why should the beaks escape? Fill out the molesworth end-of-term Report on Masters e.g.

Health: It sometimes seme that when he gaze at the skool sossages at brekfast he is not feeling well in himself. Can it hav been too much B·E·E·R the nite before? Or does he feel the same as we do about skool sossages?

General: He hav tried hard but he have still got along way to go — about 16000000000 million trillion miles would be enuff for most of us. Above all he must learn the meaning of self-D·I·S·S·I·P·L·I·N·E cheers cheers cheers. Have he any clue wot he look like when he bare his ugly fangs at a noble boy? One look would be enuff we can assure him. And wat about those yelow socks and that tie? Pull yorself together feloro and make an effort.

Signed: N. Molesworth

Next term begin on Jan 20 th but do not bother to come back.

4

HO FOR THE HOLS

GOODBY TO SKOOL
(for a bit.)

'Boys,' sa headmaster GRIMES, smiling horibly, 'st. custard's hav come to the end of another term.'

Can there be a note of relief in his craked voice? There can be no doubt of the feelings of the little pupils. CHEERS! HURRAH! WHIZZ-O! CHARGE! TA-RAN-TA-RA! The little chaps raise the roof of big skool, which do not take much doing as most of it is coming off already.

'Ah, molesworth,' bellow GRIMES to molesworth 2, who is dancing a hornpipe on a desk, 'not *too* much excitement. We hav not broken up yet, dere boy.'

'Wot, sir?'

'Not too much excite –'

'Speak up, sir.'

'GET DOWN OFF THAT FLIPPING DESK OR YOU WILL GET 6!'

At last, order is restored and end of term marks are read chiz chiz chiz. Another loud cheer greet the fakt that i am botom in eng. fr. geom. geog. div. algy and hist. When grabber get his ushaul prize i.e. the mrs joyful prize for rafia work there are boos and catcalls nothing can stop the mitey upsurge of popular feeling.

'SILENCE!' below GRIMES. 'You are unfare. You kno how he won this prize.'

'Sure!' we roar, '£5 to you, £1 all round to the staff and a botle of beer for the olde matronne. The same story.'

'SILENCE OR I WILL KANE THE LOT!'

Methinks his unatural benevolence is waring as thin as peason's second-best pare of trousis. The mob is hushed by this thort.

'Now see here,' sa GRIMES, 'see here, scum. We gives you edducation here, see? We gives you maners and disscipline, don't we? Don't forget them when you gets 'ome. Do not forget to sa "pardon" at some breach of etikette and tuck the old serviet into the colar firmly. Should egg be droped upon the tie remove same quietly with the thumb as you 'av seen me do. Be a credit to St. custards! DISMISS!'

With one mad yell the mob, armed with stumps and bits torn from desks, surge away down the pasage, trampling the masters under foot. A buket of water fall on GRIMES and the term end in a series of wizard rags and japes. Cars arive, driven by parents with drawn, white faces. The rolls for grabber, a bentley for peason and a cranky old grid for fotherington-tomas. For the rest it is the old skool bus for the station.

'Six quid,' hiss the driver to GRIMES, 'and i'll put the lot over a cliff.'

'And deprive me of my living?'

'You hav yore jellied eels and the whelk stall in the new cross road, not to mention other enterprises.'

'Begone, tempter!'

With a roar the skool bus drive off. Goodby, sir, goodby, skool, goodby, matronne, goodby, skool dog ect. No more lat. no more french. Wave wave and we are free.

Cheers for home and the maison molesworth! All are pleased to see us, dogs charge, cats miaouw and parot whistle poly wolly doodle. Wipe mud on carpet, change clothes, eat super cream buns and relax. So far only 62 people hav said we are taller, 96 that we are like mum, 107 that we are like pater and all hav asked if we had a good term. It is the same old story. Soon we are lying back in pater's chair, eating bullseyes.

'Wot is on the t.v. we hav nothing to do,' we sa.

'Nothing,' sa the parot, 'the programmes are lousy' he is browned off becos since we hav a t.v. he hav not been able to get a word in edgeways.

Mum seme to hav run out of conversation.

'Tell us about skool,' she sa, at last.

'Skool? The masters are all teddy boys and would slit you with a broken botle for 2 pins. The food is uneatable and conditions are vile.'

'You poor darlings!'

'It is horible,' blub molesworth 2.

'My poor little lambs ect' hem-hem rather embarassing mum look as if she will burst into tears, good old mum. All mums are the same and luv there wee ones somebody hav got to, after all. I send her for my mail and litely thumb over the leters i.e. 16 football pools, 1 bill from the bookmaker, a badge from

SKOOL! DISMISS! With one mad

the golly club, an invitation to a dance chiz and HO! wot
is this, eh?

Dere frend,
Welcome! in sending for details of the
Goliath, the Strong Man course you are opening a
new life. If you are a pigmy i can make a giant of
you with bulging mussles and HERCULEAN
strength in 6 weeks. Write at once with P.O. for
2/6.

(signed) G. Goliath.

Gosh! This is some-
thing! A new future
open up by the time
we return to skool
i can hav giant
strength.   How
wizard that will be
next term.

Scene: big skool at
st. custard's. Goliath
molesworth is un-
packing his tuck box.

PEASON: Hullo, o
weedy wet, you
hav a face like a
squished tomato.

MOLESWORTH:
(*thinks*) Poor fule,
he do not kno

ell the mob surge away down the passage

(enter sigismund the mad maths master)

SIGISMUND: Come on get cracking no talking no smoking, no entrance you are in my clutches agane.

(He striketh peason.)

MOLESWORTH: Stop! Enuff!

(sigismund aim a wicked blow with the protractors. molesworth catch them, bust them, brake an iron bar with his teeth, lift a statue of j. caesar, leap 82 feet, beat his chest, crunch a skool cake, do 2 back somersaults and aim a rabit punch at sigismund.)

MOLESWORTH: Take that.
SIGISMUND: Wow!
MOLESWORTH: And that and that and that and that –
SIGISMUND: Do not repeat yoreself.

(M. toss him over his shoulder and the bout is over. Sigismund is down for the count the crowd roars.)

At this point the dreme is interrupted.
'Would you like another cake, nigel?'
'No, thanks, mum. I hav some correspondence.'
'To whom are you writing?'
'Just to the golly club, mum. Just to the golly club.'
i write to the golly club thanking them for their good wishes. Also to Goliath for the strong man course. We shall see.

And so the hols proceed. I quarrel with molesworth 2 and he do not seme to see my point of view. Let him wate. Ocasionally there are treats e.g. gran come to see us in her 90 m.p.h. sports car and zoom about the roads which is more dangerous than the skool bus. Boys come in to pla and depart in tears. The parot see sooty on the t.v. and sa a rude word. He want to get an audition and kepe saing "Cock-a-doodle-doo" and swank he is a cock he will not get to first base. Then come the FELL DAY i.e.

dere nigel and molesworth 2

GLORIA AND HYACINTH

AT HOME

dancing 8 – 10.30. Cakes, creme buns, trifle, jelly, chocs, crackers, whisky for paters and gin for maters. Do not miss this unique ocasion.

A snip!!!!!

CURSES! me dancing with gurlies? gosh. i ring the bell for mater and issue stern protest but in vane. It will be good for me to go, she sa. Also gloria and hyacinth are such nice little gurls and i must learn to dance early before it is too late chiz chiz chiz.

Another weedy party and lots of weedy little gurls with pig tales and also some joly big ones. a nice lady come up with a knuckle duster and ask me to dance with tough baby called honoria. Cornered, i bow, take gurl by my gloved hand and draw her litely on the floor. After a few turns she speke shyly:

'This is a waltz, you big lout. You hav kicked me 5 times.'

'And, fare made, i will kick thee agane.'

'Sez you? I will do you if you do.'

'I shall do thee first, see if i do not.'

And so to the lite strains the young couples in the first flush of their youth whirl round and round to the strains of the craked gramophone. Wot young hopes and ideals are confined in these innocent breasts, wot – SPLOSH! Wot can that be? It is hyacinth who hav thrown a jelly at gloria she hav been sipping mater's gin. Gloria respond with the trifle cheers cheers cheers. 'Go it, gloria,' shout honoria, 'tear out her hare' and molesworth 2 zoom by dive bombing with eclares. A wizard confusion ranes.

'Did you enjoy the party, nigel?' sa mum when we get home.

'Oh yes,' i reply, tired but hapy. 'Altho next time you mite send us to the moulin rouge or an apache's dance hall.'

The weeks and days pass on winged feet. Soon we shall hav to think of getting our things together for the new term. Ah-me! All those pants and vests and shirts got out for another tour of duty. The happy relationship between me and molesworth 2 hav broken up in cries of 'Shall', 'Shan't'. 'You are.' 'You aren't' ect.

'Wot did you sa about the masters at yore skool, nigel?' ask mum. 'The ones who are teddy boys?'

'They would rip you with a botle for 2 pins, mater.'

'So would i,' she sa. 'So would i.'

As for Goliath i never hear from him agane. The golly club thank me for my contribution to party funds. They hav made me a golly Captain now. i must hav put the P.O. in the wrong envelope. I would rather be Goliath than a Golly Captain any day but that is life.

HEE-HEE FOR TEE-VEE

Gosh super! we hav something to contend with which no other generation hav ever had before i.e. the television cheers cheers cheers. Everbody kno wot a t.v. is it is a square box with a screen. You switch on and o hapen, then just when you hav given up hope and are going off to buzz conkers a great booming voice sa, 'That's an interesting point, postlethwaite. Wot does higginbottom feel? Higginbottom? ect ect.' It may be an interesting point but i could not care less and just go away agane when a ghastley face suddenly appere. It is worse than a squished tomato but it hold me in hypnotic trance and it is the same with molesworth 2, tho he always look dopey like that. We sit and watch more and more ghastley faces with our mouths open and even forget to chew the buble gum we are slaves of the machine.

Of course all boys and gurls hav to go through a time when there is no t.v. xcept at the postman's down the road. Yore mater and pater then sa weedy things.

i will not hav one in the house.

the programmes are simply terible, my dear.

it is bad for children.

it destroy the simple pursuits of leisure.

Hem-hem if they only knew what the simple pursuits of leisure were like potting stones at vilage oiks or teaching parot rude words they would not hesitate for a moment. Anyway they get one in the end and sa 'Children can only look for 1 hour at suitable programmes' then they forget all about it until we are halfway through '1984' and molesworth 2 sa 'if that is the best a rat can do i do not think much of it.' 'The rat,' i sa, 'is exactly like thou, o clot-faced wet.' Then mater become aware of our presence and hury the dreamy-eyed little felows up wood hill to blanket fair, as dear nana sa.

A ghastley face suddenly appere

When you setle down to it this is wot hapens in your dulce domum (lat.)

Scene: A darkened room with glowing fire. Mum, Nana, me and molesworth 2 are goggling at the screen. So are the cats, dogs, rats, mice and various bugs about the place.

T.V. Are you a clump-press minder? (Grate cheers)
MATER: I thort he was an aero-dynamicist or a moulding-clamp turner......I really think.....
ALL: Sshh!

(Enter pater, tired from the office.)

PATER: Are you looking at that friteful thing agane? Programmes are terible. Nothing to look at.

(With a roar and a ratle he put coal on the fire).

ALL: Sshh!

(Pater setle down. molesworth 2 aim his gat at very fat gentleman in specs. It is the same gun with which he shot mufin the mule, mcdonald hobley, a ping-pong champion, three midgets, a great-crested grebe, a persian student and lady Boyle and a budgerigar.)

MOLESWORTH 2. Ah-ah-ah-ah-ah. Got you.
ALL: Ssh!
MATER: Do you not think it would be better if their heads were not three feet away from their shoulders?

(Pater go and twiddle knobs. First of all there is a snowstorm then what seem like the batle of jutland, then an electronic bombardment. Finaly a vast explosion.)

MATER: You hav ruined it, clot.
NANA: Boost the contrast.
MOLESWORTH 2: Adjust the definition.
ME: O gosh, hurry up.

(Now picture is upside down, then leaning drunkenly, then it disappear altogether amid boos and catcalls. Finaly Nana do it.)

T.V. Are you conected with seaweed? (Huge cheer)
MATER: look at tibby the cat he canot stand gilbert harding.....
ALL: Sssh.
PATER: He's a guggle-gouger.....

(And so it go on. Supper is not cooked, fires go out, kettles boil their heads off, slates fall off the roof and house burn down, but we are all still looking at a nature film in w. africa chiz in fact we hav seen more monkeys since we got the t.v. than ever before xcept at st. custard's where peason hav the face of a wild baboon.)

He is going to zoom to the piano and pla fairy bells

Aktually t.v. is v. cultural for boys and improving to the mind. You learn so many things that when you go back to skool all are quite surprised.

MOLESWORTH 1. To the q. whether the hydrogen bomb should be banned i give a categorical 'no'. unless there can be international agreement to co-exist in disarmament.

MOLESWORTH 2: That is a valid point, o weedy wet. Do you kno the population of chile?

MOLESWORTH 1: No. But everyone should look both ways before crossing the road and wot can be more dramatic than man's fight against the locust, eh?

MOLESWORTH 2: The problem of asia is the problem of over-population and now i will pla brahams etude number 765000 in F flat.....

You kno wot this mean he is going to zoom to the piano and pla fairy bells nothing can stop him the whole skool will rock and plaster drop from the ceiling, chandeliers will shake and light bulbs burst. Hav to take cover until it is all over when the head of an elk, dislodged by the blast, fall on my head chiz chiz chiz that is life.

So you will see that t.v. is a joly good thing and very restful to the nerves, my dear. You can talk about it next day, particularly to those who hav no sets and hav not seen the programmes. This make you very popular socially, with the smart set of 3B, and take your mind off the lessons. It also gives rise to several wizard wheezes. For instance, why not start a maths lesson with a ghastley face smiling at you?

'And now, 3B, we are going to show you the elementary principles of vulgar fractions so we hope simper simper you will be able simper to get the things into yore thick heads without carving the desk or sticking compasses into fotherington-Tomas. Simper. May we also remind you that there is cocoa and buns at break and from 10.30 to 11.15 there is a gorgeous lesson in which Cotta will be beaten for the umpteenth time by the Belgians with darts and arows?'

With a huge SIMPER the picture fade. Which only leave time to prepare placard for the final wizard wheeze.

molesworth, next sentence. Marcus and Balbus, my dearest friends, are walking out of the city. Come along, boy.

You do not need to sa er-er and scratch yore head or even ask what the blazes the two cissies are doing walking out of the city for. You just hoist your placard for a technical hitch:

> NORMAL SERVICE
> WILL BE RESTORED
> AS SOON AS POSS.

A NEW DEAL FOR THE TINIES

Hist! Cave! methinks the bold bad molesworth 1 have wind that there are tinies around the place. you kno wot tinies are – they are ickle pritty little boys who wear blue corduroy trousis and zoom about on fairy cycles. They hav not come to st custard's yet they do not kno their fate. They hav mistresses at skool and dance weedily with ickle gurls chiz chiz chiz e.g.

Now david, now bobby, now cyril stand round me in a fairy ring and join hands with drusilla we will pretend we are all going to fairyland.

At this all the tinies becom xcited and jump up and down. Goody goody hurray and hip hip they cri shall we see a fairy godmother?

'But,' sa fotherington-Tomas, when i express these things to him, 'we must hav the younger tinies to folow in our footsteps. After all,' he sa, 'you were a tiny once yourself.'

'Me? Curses!'

'With corduroy trousis and your mother wept when she cut off your curls. You looked just like bubbles, molesworth 1, and the old ladies said how swete you were.'

With that he skip weedily away singing tra-la-tra-la but i feel there is a grane of truth in wot he sa. Gosh chiz, i dare not think of it. Me in corduroy trousis! 10000000000 boos to bubbles.

Aktually all boys hav to hav a time when they are not tuough and canot even read. There was even a time when i had no culture myself hem-hem which was when my pater and mater thort i was a brane and would win a skolarship. Not much hope of making *me* a slave to pay the fees nowadays. But there was a time once when –

(Scene) the molesworth nursery young nigel molesworth is sitting on the floor braking a hornby trane with a hamer. The

There was even a time when i had no culture myself

place is litered with debris of wheels nuts bolts dinky toys tanks and clockwork mice it is as if there hav been an H-bomb xplosion.

NURSE: come nigel dere it is time for your reading lesson.
NIGEL: Boo-hoo-boo-hoo-hoo.
NURSE: If you are wilful i will smak yore little hand.
NIGEL: And i will thro the hamer at you. If you want to get tuough, you can hav it tuough dere nana.

(With a quick judo thro nana come up from behind and disposess the game little chap of his weapon. He sits upon her ample knee with an open book.)

It is a funy thing about reading when you are a tiny they make you sa Ah-Eh-Ih-Ou-URR etc. which is uterly wet and read about weedy dogs e.g.

There is a dog. Jack is a . . . Jack is a . . . Jack is a . . . is a bitch. No, not that, nigel, do not guess. Read the word. Wot does DER-OU-GER spell? Jack is a dog he is a bad dog jack steals the bone . . . (zoom zoom along you can remember it all). Cook is angry. Cook is a cow. Well, that is what dere Dada . . . Cook is a lady. She whacks jack with the LUR-AH-DUR-LUR-ER. Wot the blazes can that be? She whacks jack with the hamer . . . with the gun . . . with the cosh . . . with the rolling pin . . . etc. etc. And so it go on until nana fall into a stupor and it is time for the archer family on the wireless.

Everything is difficult for tinies they hav to write too. But first they pla with plastissene and make drawings in crayons which is like glorious tecknicolour hem-hem i don't think. When they write it is like this they copy things *why dus the owl owl wod pek on the nos.* Or, *hokey-de-poke de zoopity zing you are under my spel and dus everything i tell.*

wot speling eh?

Soon however the tinies can use their new found skill and scrible on their books rude things about lambs, roy the rat, tortoises, geese which they hav to read about e.g. *ded he is ded i shot him he is ded yes.* This show promise for the future and a brite career at st custards.

Another thing tinies kno o about is games such as foop-ball or criket. When they first see a foopball they are amazed. 'What do we do with it?' they ask the mistress. 'You slam the leather right-footed into the reticule, little dears,' she repli. So they put the ball down and retire to the end of the field then zoom up for huge shot. Ball go two inches and tiny fall on his nose. 'Ha-ha-ha,' sa mistress, 'that will teach you, rat. Now it is cedric's turn.'

It is the same with criket, which the tinies ushually learn with their pater on the lawn.

pater: Set up the stumps, boys.

Do you not want to be grown-up?

tiny: i were playing with my balloon.

pater: All grown-up men pla criket. Do you not want to be grown-up?

tiny: not when i see some grown-up men, Dada.

But pater is inexorable. He grasps the bat. First tiny bowls the ball backwards over his head, then into the greenhouse, then along the ground and finaly the dog run away with it. When the pill is recovered tiny bowl pater with a wizard daisy-cutter. Pater then bowl and hit tiny's stumps. 'You're out!' he yells. Tiny throw the bat at him and walk off into the house. The game is over.

So you see. Even the Hugest hav been tinies once. And even when they are huge and hairy as me their maters sometimes sa: 'Did I show you that sweet photo of nigel when he was a baby?' And there you are looking weedy on a rug. But it's all right as long as none of the other boys don't see. You take another look. You weren't a bad looking tiny at all quite d. in that peticoat – curses wot am i saing?

Dere Little Chaps

Will you take me for
a bike ride, dad?

Parkins shows a good deal
of promise.

nigel is a slo developer.

You hav caught me, sir, like a treen in a disabled space ship.

i shouldn't do that if i were you, old chap.

SUMER BY THE SEA

Hurra for the hols agane cheers cheers cheers. Boo and snubs to all skools and masters which are closed for repairs and renovation during august. ('i think we'll have big skool done a pale dove grey with petunia lame curtains,' sa headmaster's wife hem-hem i do not think. Big skool will be lucky if it get a rinse with the carbolic.)

Wot will the little chaps do with themselves when they can no longer wake up each day in their beloved alma mater? (SKOOL! SKOOL! SKOOL! BASH 'EM UP ST CUSTARD'S!) Wot will they do, eh? Frankly i would hardly like to sa it is so unspekeable wot with 3 cokes and $\frac{1}{2}$ a lb of home-made fudge before 10 a.m.

A few, however, of the more thortful types will be planing ahead for lazy days by the sea e.g.

'i see that striped beachwear is in fashion agane this season,' sa molesworth 2, laing down his ladies mag hem-hem. 'Do you intend to be chic this season molesworth 1 in casual slashnecked coton with delectable acessories or do you intend to wear your ushual dirty blue drawers?'

'Shutup molesworth 2 i am looking at t.v.'

't.v. is the curse of modern youth. Wot is on?'

'It is a brany chap who hav made a telescope out of a tin of pineaple chunks as a sparetime hoby.'

(3 *hours later. plus* 2 *mins and* 6 *secs.*)

'The pla is over and i have guesed that it was an etruscan jam jar dated circa 1066a.d.,' sa molesworth 2. 'Where shall we all go for our glamorous holiday in the sun? Shall it be breezy ventnor? or rolicking ryde? Do you wish to find health and hapiness at bridlington molesworth one? Perhaps romance will come your way this year, o weedy wet. Or do you prefer the s. of france?'

'Ah how joli et gai the s. of france would be!'

(*He dreameth.*)

La France. Beneath an orange umbrela sit molesworth 1 *on a chaise on the terace of the hotel magnifique. there is the scent of jasmin and bullseyes in the air, an orchestra pla the minstrel boy softly, Le soleil brille. molesworth turn to his companion, the glamorous hortense –*

M. MOLESWORTH: j'aime voo, hortense.

HORTENSE: Oo la-la and houp-la. c'est vrai?

M. MOLESWORTH: (*souriant soppily*) Les loups sont laids, les elephants sont enormes, les girafes sont hauts.

HORTENSE: Wot the blazes hav that got to do with it, mon amour?

M. MOLESWORTH: it is all the fr. i can remember it is potts and pilcher fr. primer ex 9B and wot is a grate surprise to all is that all the adjs hav an 's'.

HORTENSE: Why do you always hav to bring the loups into it? The loups are idiotics. they are unnecessaries. they are humides. they are weedys they are unintelligents. (*She brake off and stares*) Qui est ce beau gars?

m'sieu molesworth regard autour de lui.

M. MOLESWORTH: Mon dieu c'est grabber the tete de la skool! Je l'ai eu (i hav had it). *He gives another quick blow of the eye.* Non, j'ai tort egad c'est M. Hubert our fr. master –

M. Hubert sees molesworth and reels with dismay. i supose it is hard chedar when you come on a cheap pleasure hol and find me there large as life at the other end. Any case in certain circumstances masters seem to feel boys cramp their style e.g. over GURLS.

M. HUBERT. Cor cripes its molesworth i must get the blazes out of here. (*Il voit hortense*) Well this is reel nice, molesworth, is the lady votre mere?

HORTENSE: Mais essayez-vous clot et dites moi qui vous etes etc?

La France. Beneath an orange umbrela sit molesworth

a chaise on the terace of the hotel magnifique

HUBERT: Come again?

M. MOLESWORTH: She was telling you to sit down and give an account of yourself. Pray join us.

(*the fr. master so betwitched with the beauty of hortense that he take molesworth's hand and kiss it chiz chiz chiz.*)

MOLESWORTH: As i was saing the loups sont laids.....

But it is no use hortense and the fr. master gaze into each other's eyes. Finaly armand the boy from the fr. book appear with Papa. Houp-la he sa i see the sea. Big boats go on the sea. Is the sea wet?

PAPA: Non armand but you are.

He push him quietly off the port and join the fr. master and hortense. The dream fades.....

Aktually most boys do not get the chance of a happy hol in the s. of France. They go on the broads where a steady percentage fall in and are never heard of agane: they go in caravans or camps, they are sent to aged aunts who hav houses au bord de la mer. Anything to save money.

molesworth 2 and me ushually get a lite sentence at a boarding house at Babbling-by-sea e.g.

MON REPOS

frunished accommodation
teas. new laid eggs.
letuces from own garden.
piano taught. Manicure.

Prop. Mrs furbelow.
(aply within)

Mon repos is a pritty tuough place and make even st.
custard's seem like the ritz. It always rain when we arive and
all in a bad temper. Inside front door is a mat which sa
'*Welcom*' and a huge hairy lady spring out at us and below
'*Wipe your shoes*'. In fact this is all you are alowed to do in
mon repos the rest e.g. sliding down banisters, having
baths, bunging cushions etc is stricktly forbidden. There is
no future in wiping your shoes forever so it is beter to brave
the elements outside.

You kno how they describe hols in the childrens books
e.g. as soon as mummy and daddy had unpacked the eager
little chaps ran off with their bukets and spades to the sea-
shore. If you do this at babblington-on-sea you get blown
sixty miles inland the wind is so ferce. You hav to hang on
all the way if you want to get down to the beach.

And then wot do you see? Babies. Nothing but babies.
Some sit in pudles, some stager drunkenly across the sand,
some beat pat a cake with a spade but most just sit there with
their mouths open looking loopy. And when you pass it is
always the same thing the mum sa: 'Baby sa helo to the nice
little boy.' Me nice? Hem-hem.

'But you were,' sa molesworth 2, weedily. 'my first
recolection as i opened my blue baby eyes was you molesworth 1 you were shaking a ratle and sa ickle pritty
brudder.'

'i was only saing my lines.'

'That may be but mum always sa i was a beautiful baby.'

'time molesworth 2 works grate changes.'

Ho for beach criket! As the tide recede leaving vast
expanse of seaweed, old bottles, planks and oil wot can be
nicer than a joly game of criket? All the fathers encourage
their little ones and the little ones gaze at their fathers with
their white hary legs and become depresed about the future.
If we are all to grow up like that wot is the use of going on,
eh? Paters are oblivious of this and encourage all.

'Come on cyril you are in...don't blub...timothy

is not blubing...hit a six old chap...well tried...next man ect ect ect ect.... until all the children are blubing and all the paters are plaing it is the same old story. Wot is left for the new boyhood? They dash into the sea with glad cries and drown themselves. So boo to boarding houses, cliffs, bukets, spades, water wings, windmills, model boats seaweed and striped beachwear – roll on thou grate and restless ocean roll over the LOT.

Roll on thou grate and restless ocean roll over the LOT

5

THE CRUEL HARD WORLD

WHO WILL BE WOT?

Fellow weeds, hav you ever cast those blue eyes of yours – just like your mater's hem-hem – into the grimy future? Wot i mean is, we are YOUTH chiz chiz whether we like it or not and as every weed who come to give us prizes sa – The Future is in yore Keeping.

n.b. it is no use saing We don't want it. You can keep it etc. *Nobody* wants the future and we are left holding the baby chiz chiz chiz.

These Grate and FEARLESS thorts come to me the other day in prep as i stare gloomily at the imperfect subjunk of avoir. From that i allow my gaze to wander out of the window at those little feathered creatures who kno tru freedom. Next i draw a wizard H-bomb xplosion and then i look around me at my felow weeds.

All these oiks, tuoughs, weeds, wets, bulies, snekes, cads, dolts and knaves – Wot will Become of Them?

Hav they tried their best? No. Hav they put the Subjekt in the Nom? No! Hav they kept their eye on the pill at criket? No! Hav they been well-manered and respecktful to the masters? No! Hav they heeded warnings and pi-jaws? Absolutely not!

Wot is to become of them? The molesworth Daydream Service now merged with Bets, Wagers and Prophesies Inc. produce the answer.

o89281 GRABBER. Everyone kno grabber he is head of the skool and winner of the mrs joyful prize for rafia work.

He also win every other prize and is collosally rich etc. Everyone now would sa wot a bright future lies before him, the world is at his feet. Ah no, the grate buly hav an ugly fate. First, his pater lose all his money so grabber drift from bad to worse and as he could not be worse now this is joly difficult. First it is the pin-table halls, then pepsi-cola, then dogs, then GURLS and then horses. In fact the only good thing to be said of this wastrel product was that he liked the horses better than the gurls.

In the end a mere empty husk grabber came back one night to st. custard's, the scene of his brilliant triumps as a youth. He climb in through the ushual window and gaze at the darkened classrooms. Alas, the scene do not soften his callous soul. No tears glisten in those beady eyes. In the morning the skool come down and gaze open-mouthed at the Blakboard. Some words hav been rudely chalked hem-hem.

LATIN IS SOPPY. MATHS ARE MAD. FRENCH IS FRITEFUL. ALG IS AWFUL. WOODWORK IS WET. THE FOOD COULD DO WITH IMPROVEMENT.

This terible crime so shoked the nation that the whole resources of Scotland Yard were thrown into tackling the criminal. grabber was caught and sent to Wormwood scrubs were he met several old custardians. The governor put him straight on to rafia work ignorant that this had been the cause of his downfall. Soon the inmates were shoked by another outrage in the Health and Beauty Hall.

WARDERS ARE WEEDS. GOVERNORS ARE GURLIES. RAFIA WORK IS ROTEN. THE CELLS ARE DISGRACEFUL AND THE FOOD COULD DO WITH IMPROVEMENT.

The eye of the prophet molesworth

For this grabber get another 7 years but he sa he do not care so boo there is no difrence between st. custard's and wormwood scrubs anyway.

The eye of the prophet molesworth next lite upon dere little fotherington-Tomas. Wot does the cristal ball reveal for this gurly? Can it be true? AIR VICE-MARSHAL SIR BASIL FOTHERINGTON-TOMAS, V.C., D.S.O. Clubs: Spaceman's, Ovalteenies.

Air Vice-Marshal Sir basil fotherington-Tomas lowered himself into the cockpit of the gleaming space jet (complete with all parts £2 mill.)

Is the atomic reactor set to zero, Huggins?
Yessir.
Anti-gravity boosters to half-cock?
Yessir.
Pressure reading $8\frac{1}{2}$?
Yessir.
Radial dynaflow in parallel?
Yessir.
That's it then. Can't afford to make a mistake. Only a fifty-fifty chance I'll make mercury. So long, Huggins.

SHoo-SHoo-SHoo
ooooooooooooooooooooooooooooooo
oooooooooooooSH

OBITUARY. (*By a pal.*)

All those who knew basil fotherington-Tomas will mourn the death of a very brave space pioneer. He won a v.c. for shooting down 99 spaceships off mars and this was folowed by the d.s.o. for beating up the bauxite in Betelgeuse. Sir basil was educated at st. custard's where he is still remembered for his skipping and liteness of foot. 'He skipped everything,' said his head-master, reminiscently.....

O goody sa fotherington-Tomas peeping over my shoulder
O goody molesworth you hav put me in and made me brave.
How can i thank you enuff? i'm brave i'm brave hurra.
I should not count on it, i sa. It is only a flite of fancy.
Thanks all the same. You are super molesworth 1 you really are. Now wot is yore future?

Another splendid creation by NIGEL

Who me oh i sa gosh no.
Fearfully i put my grate nose towards the cristal ball....

Another splendid creation by NIGEL is this
daring cocktail frock in burned orange and
squashed muskrat. Note how Nigel has modelled
bodice and waist in crashed chipmunk and a
flaring skirt with matching beads. No wonder
that Nigel's B-line is the sensation of the season.
Nigel has *flair*! Nigel will be showing his spring
colection.....

CURSES! I take the wretched cristal pill and punt it out
of the window. It take few things to drive me back to the
imperfect subjunk of avoir but this is one of them. J'eusses
tu euse..... But wot's the good of any of it?

WORKER No. 12345/C NYE MOLESWORTH

5 rats eat 6 seed cakes in 43 mins, 9 secs. They pause for twenty minutes. Then they eat 29 rock cakes in 15 secs (dead). They pause for 1 minute, 13 secs. Then they eat a cheese in 33 minutes.

How long do the rats take to eat the seed cakes, the rock cakes and the cheese?

Wot a question, eh, to ask a boy! But that's the sort of thing you get faced with in exams and if you don't pass exams in this brave age you DON'T GET ON. chiz. Of corse it is quite easy to see why a weed who kno the height of Ben Nevis also that vertically oposite angles are equal is a beter bet for a bank or dog biscuit firm than me who kno o less than o cheers cheers cheers. But wot ocasionally depress me in my few leisure moments, my dear, is that you hav to go on taking exams all through your life chiz chiz chiz chiz
  e.g.

THE BOSS: Ah, fotherington-Tomas, wot is the population of grater london eh?
F-TOMAS: 44 million and a few odd thou.
THE BOSS: Are the oposite sides of a parallelogram equal?
F-TOMAS: Indeed they are, sir.
THE BOSS: i won't ask you about the rats. . . . you hav satisfied me. You are now export manager.
F-TOMAS: O goody!

You see wot i mean? Except for a couple of peaceful years doing national service the brave new clots hav got nothing but EXAMS EXAMS EXAMS. And it's the same for the gurls, too.

Aktually there is one comfort for clots like me who are not brany we can always get a job in a factory. In fact factories are glad to get anybody to judge from their notices:

```
┌─────────────────────────────────────────────┐
│                                             │
│   BLITHERING M'FAKTURING COY                │
│                 WANTED                       │
│   Toggle adjusters, clump press minders, tigglers, │
│   snorer hoisters, glug drillers, swarf wipers, │
│   troggers and cricks.                       │
│   SKILLED, SEMI-SKILLED, CLOTS, MENTALLY    │
│   DEFICIENT. IDIOTS, NUMSKULLS.             │
│          ALL WELCOME.                        │
│   CANTEEN,  PENSION,  PROFIT  SHARING,      │
│   SONGS  AT  THE  PIANO.  FREE  SHAMPOO.    │
│   SHADY TERACES. ALL WELCOME                 │
│      AND WE PAY YOU FOR IT, TOO!            │
│                                             │
└─────────────────────────────────────────────┘
```

O.K. No need to wory if you canot pass your Eleven Plus or Comon Entrance to an extremely tuough public skool, all you hav to do is to wait until you are 15 and cash in at the dere old plant.

This is wot hapen. You catch the old works bus and clock-in, put on your overalls, chaff the gurls, turn on the air conditioning, open the marshmallows and switch on the old precision tool. Any fool kno how to work a precision tool it's pappy. You feed in a piece of steel at one end and the machine grab it, hoist it over, punch, turn it back, punch it, press it, heave it upside down make a right-hand thread, squeeze it in two and there you have a finished snibber ready to rivet into the crocks of the cramp thus marrying the prip with the creech in the finished end-product.

But wot make work in the factory so fasscinating is the GOOD CONVERSATION in the shops. Effie on the glug driller next door tell you all that she sa to her boy-friend last nite and you tell her wot you see on the telly you've just bought and all the machines go –

A puff-a grab – sizzle – grunt – screeeeeee – ow – gosh – sizzle – screeeee – ow – help – gosh – and agane – screeeeee——

In fact, all are happy turning out milions of snibbers when in come the shop foreman.

All right, he sa, switch off we're downing tools. Send for the manager and quick. Tell him I'm waiting. Jump to it, molesworth, i just seen another nine snibbers drop off. If you're not careful they'll be making a profit.

'Wot,' you sa, throing an oily rag at Effie, 'seems to be the trouble, horace?'

'Felow called peason without a union card in the paint shop. Manager won't sack him so i am calling you out.'

So it's no more snibbers and out with the old cards and a nice game of pontoon. Pity really becos it's not as if you were doing much work in the first place. Anyway imagine wot it would be like if this sort of thing spreads –

Scene 3B. Master is reading his ushual book of love and passion while form swot at fr. verbs, dab criket, NOUGHTS and crosses, pools, free verse and other trifles of the boy mind.

Enter GILLIBRAND, *foaming at the mouth.*

GILLIBRAND: All right. That's enuff. We're out. Down yore potts and pilcher fr. primer.

BEAK: (*reciting dreamily*) She galoped across the desert hem-hem in his strong tawny arms . . . . . (*he gives a start*) Wot is the meaning of this?

GILLIBRAND: a stoppage.

BEAK: No no, not that. How ghastley! Let the production lines of avoir, etre, donner, aimer and recevoir roll on. After all, you're a reasonable boy. (*thinks*: i must be polite to the twirp tho i would like to give him six).

GILLIBRAND: a tick in 1B hav exceeded his algy quota yesterday. We can't hav that, you kno.

The Beak fall down on his knees.

it is by such an example as i, like those other brave, clear-eyed workers
in the documentary films that britain will win its export batle

BEAK: Don't go out. Stay on the jobs. i'll do anything to put this injustice right ect. ect.

Well, imagine that if poss. There is a grate deal of thortful work to be done on labour relations between beaks and boys though i expect it will be the same old story do wot you're told or 6 of the best.

Back to the factory now and 12345/c nye molesworth hav been shifted from the machine shop and is now working in asembly as a reward for his zeal promise and enthusiasm. Let us prick our grimy ears and listen. The forman speaketh.

'molesworth!'

'wot me? it was me the last time.'

'you 'eard. get up there, lad, and give it a $\frac{3}{8}$ turn on the left-hand creep. Why you looking like that?'

'Nothink. i wasn't looking – i was thinking. it's ten to twelve, that's all. Time i get up i'll hav to come down. don't seem any sense in it, really.'

'Any other thorts?'

'it's hot-pot today. Always hot-pot at the canteen thurs-days. ho well, i'll get on down to the stores now – '

'waffor?'

'draw a $\frac{3}{8}$ monkey. i can't look at the job without a $\frac{3}{8}$ monkey now can i and if the creep is crabbing i'll need a blower and talking of blowers – '

'i kno. 12 o'clock and hot-pot thursdays. The trubble with you, molesworth – '

Hoooooooooooooooooooooooooooooooooooooo.....!

it is by such an example as i stand there like those other brave, clear-eyed workers in the documentary films that britain will win its export batle hem-hem i do not think. But you hav to be careful. you don't want to do too well tho or you may become a manager and hav to recieve reports from head ofice e.g.

Be careful or you may become a manager

PRODUCTION: very disapointing. why?
RAW MATERIALS: very disapointing.
    See tomkins.
LABOUR POSITION: very disapointing.

in fact it is just like a skool report or one of mine at any rate and it would seme that you go on having reports as well as exams all yore life. Wot an outlook. fancy giving us all that free milk and orange juice just for that. still if we all work hard enuff they are promising the workers automatick nuclear atommic factories which do all the work by themselves. cheers cheers. Then the problem is LEAISURE. cheers. Well, leaisure hav never been any problem to me – and now yore rolls-royce is at the machine shop door, mr molesworth. O.K. – and hav this precision tool gold-plated by the time i return tomorrow. Exit the wealthy worker 12345/c nye molesworth and all the machines go:

A puff-a grab – sizzle – grunt – screee – ow – gosh – sizzle – screeeeee – ect.

Produktivity in Skool

The molesworth production line for latin sentences

1 The raw sentence is fed into the sorter

2 The words pass along an endless belt into the electronik dicker

3 The dicker disgorges
them as latin

4 The assembler puts
them together

5 The boys take them to the ticking machine

Snip! Snip! Snip!!!!!!!!!!!!!!!!

At speshul sacrifice!!!!

HEADMASTER FOR SALE

Small, part used in fare condition considering. Mustache recently trimmed and shoes soled with ruber excelent for cobbing boys, miscreants ect.

No maintenance. Can live on seaweed and thinks boys can, too.

Handy, adjustable, can be used for any purpose. Cantilever movement.

together with

SET OF KANES (part-worn and frayed)

price one d. or offer

or

would exchange for jumping flea